Abortion Bibliography

For 1970

Abortion Bibliography
For 1970

compiled by
Mary K. Floyd

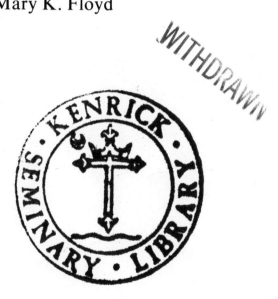

Whitston Publishing Company
Incorporated
Troy, New York
1972

PREFACE

Abortion Bibliography for 1970 is the first annual list of books and articles surrounding the subject of abortion in the preceeding year. It will appear serially each fall hereafter as a contribution toward documenting in one place as comprehensively as possible one of our central social issues.

Searches in compiling this material have covered the most widely diverse and disparate sources: *Books in Print; Bibliographic Index; Canadian Periodical Index; Cumulative Book Index; Cumulative Index to Nursing Literature; Current Index to Journals in Education; Current Literature of Venereal Disease; Education Index; Index to Legal Periodicals; Index Medicus; Index to Periodical Articles Related to Law; International Nursing Index; Public Affairs Information Service; Readers Guide to Periodical Literature; Social Sciences and Humanities Index.*

The bibliography is divided into two sections: a title section in alphabetical order; and a subject section. Thus, if the researcher does not wish to observe the subject heads of the compiler, he can use the title section exclusively. The 63 subject heads, however, have been allowed to issue from the nature of the material indexed rather than, for example, being imposed from Library of Congress subject heads or other standard lists.

LIST OF ABBREVIATIONS

ABBREVIATIONS	TITLE
ACOG Nurses Bull	ACOG Nurses Bulletin (Chicago)
AJN or Amer J Nurs	American Journal of Nursing (New York)
AORN J	AORN Journal (Engelwood, Colorado)
Acta Obstet Gynec Scand	Acta Obstetricia et Gynecologica Scandinavica (Lund)
Acta Paedopsychiatr	Acta Paedopsychiatrica (Basel)
Adelaide L Rev	Adelaide Law Review (Adelaide)
Advances Metab Dis	Advances in Metabolic Disorders (New York)
Akush Ginek	Akusherstvo i Ginekologiia (Moscow)
Akush Ginek or Akush Ginekol (Sofiia)	Akusherstvo i Ginekologiia (Sofiia) formerly Akusherstvo i Ginekologiia; supplement to Suvremenna Meditsina (Sofiia)
Ala J Med Sci	Alabama Journal of Medical Sciences (Birmingham)
Am U L Rev	American University Law Review (Washington, D.C.)
America	America (San Francisco)
American Academy of Political and Social Science	American Academy of Political and Social Science Annals (Philadelphia)
Amer J Obstet Gynec	American Journal of Obstetrics and Gynecology (St. Louis)
Amer J Psychiat or Am J Psychiatry	American Journal of Psychiatry (Hanover, N.H.)
American Legion Mag	American Legion Magazine (New York)
Anesthesiology	Anesthesiology (Philadelphia)
Ann Chir	Annales de Chirurgie (Paris)
Ann Medicopsychal	Annales Medico-Psychologiques (Paris)
Ann NY Acad Sci	Annals of the New York Academy of Sciences (New York)
Arch Gen Psychiatry	Archives of General Psychiatry (Chicago)
Aust NZ J Obstet Gynaecol	Australian and New Zealand Journal of Obstetrics and Gynaecology (Melbourne)

Bordeaux Med	Bordeaux Medical (Bordeaux)
Br Med J	British Medical Journal (London)
Bull Fed Gynec Obstet Franc or Bull Fed Soc Gynecol Obstet Lang Fr	Bulletin de la Federation des Societes de Gynecologie et d'Obstetrique de Langue Francaise (Paris)
Bull Infirm Cathol Can	Bulletin des Infirmieres Catholiques du Canada (Quebec)
Bull NY Acad Med	The New York Academy of Medicine Bulletin (New York)
Bull Soc Sci Med Grand Duche Luxemb	Societe des Sciences Medicales du Grand-Duche de Luxembourg Bulletin (Luxembourg)
CR Acad Sci	Comptes Rendus herdomadaires des Seances de l'Academie des Sciences; D: Sciences Naturelles (Paris)
CR Soc Biol	Comptes Rendus des Seances de la Societe de Biologie et de ses Filiales (Paris)
Calif Med	California Medicine (San Francisco)
Canad Med Ass J	Canadian Medical Association Journal (Toronto)
Canad Nurse	Canadian Nurse (Ottawa)
Can Forum	Canadian Forum (Ontario)
Can Ment Hlth	Canada's Mental Health (Ottawa)
Cath Nurse	Catholic Nurse (Bristol, England)
Cath World	Catholic World (Paramus, New Jersey)
Cesk Gynec	Ceskoslovenska Gynekologie (Prague)
Chatelaine	Chatelaine (Toronto)
Child Welfare	Child Welfare (New York)
Chr Cent	Christian Century (Chicago)
Chr Today	Christianity Today (Washington, D.C.)
Clin Obstet Gynecol	Clinical Obstetrics and Gynecology (New York)
Columbia Forum	Columbia Forum (New York)
Commonweal	Commonweal (New York)
Cong Q W Rept	Congressional Quarterly Service: Weekl Report (Washington)
Conn Med	Connecticut Medicine (New Haven)
Crim L R	Criminal Law Review (London)
Dan Med Bull	Danish Medical Bulletin (Kobenhavn)
Deutsch Med Wschr	Deutsch Medizinische Wochenschrift (Stutgart)

Dick L Rev	Dickinson Law Review (Lincoln, Nebraska)
Dtsch Gesundheitsw	Deutsche Gesundheitswesen (Berlin)
Duadecim	Duadecim (Helsinki)
Duquesne L Rev	Duquesne University Law Review (Pittsburgh)
Economist	Economist (London)
Editorial Res Rpts	Editorial Research Reports (Washington)
Fam Coordinator	Family Coordinator (Minneapolis)
Family Planning Perspectives	Family Planning Perspectives (New York)
Feldsh Akush	Fel'dsker I Akusherka (Moscow)
Fordham L Rev	Fordham Law Review (New York)
Ga L Rev	Georgia Law Review (Macon)
Geburtshilfe Frauen- heilkd	Geburtshilfe Frauenheilkunde (Stutgart)
Ginecol Obstet Mex	Ginecologia y Obstetricia de Mexico (Mexico City)
Ginek Pol	Ginekologia Polska (Lodz)
Good H	Good Housekeeping (New York)
Gynec Prat	Gynecologie Pratique (Paris)
Harefauh	Harefauh (Tel Aviv)
Harper's	Harper's (New York)
Harv Civil Rights L Rev	Harvard Civil Rights - Civil Liberties Law Review (Cambridge)
Hawaii Med J	Hawaii Medical Journal (Honolulu)
Hosp Med	British Journal of Hospital Medicine (London)
Hospitals	Hospitals (Chicago)
Humangenetik	Humangenetik (Berlin)
Imprint	Imprint (New York)
Indian J Public Health	Indian Journal of Public Health (Calcutta)
Int J Fertil	International Journal of Fertility (Springfield, Massachusetts)
Int Surg	International Surgery (Chicago)
Israeli Reports to the Eighth International Congress of Com- parative Law	Israeli Reports to the Eighth Internation- al Congress of Comparative Law (Tel Aviv)
JAMA	Journal of the American Medical Association (Chicago)

J Biosoc Sci	Journal of Biosocial Science (London)
J Endocr	Journal of Endocrinology (London)
J Family L	Journal of Family Law (Louisville, Kentucky)
J Infect Dis	Journal of Infectious Diseases (Chicag
J Iowa Med Soc	Journal of the Iowa Medical Society (D Moines)
J Jap Med Assoc	Journal of the Japan Medical Associat (Tokyo) in Japanese: Nippon Ishikai Zasshi
J Jap Obstet Gynec Soc	Journal of the Japanese Obstetrical an Gynecological Society (Tokyo) in Japanese: Nippon Sanka - Fujinka Gakkai Zasshi
J Kans Med Soc	Journal of the Kansas Medical Society (Topeka)
J Kentucky Med Ass	Journal of the Kentucky Medical Association (Louisville)
J La State Med Soc	Journal of the Louisiana State Medical Society (New Orleans)
J Med Assoc Ga	Journal of the Medical Association of Georgia (Atlanta)
J Med Assoc State Ala	Journal of the Medical Association of the State of Alabama (Montgomery)
J Med Lab Technal	Journal of Medical Laboratory Technol (London)
J Med Liban	Journal Medical Libanais: Lebanese Medical Journal (Beirut)
J Mississippi Med Ass	Journal of the Mississippi State Medic Association (Jackson)
J Nat Med Ass	Journal of the National Medical Assoc tion (New York)
J Nerv Ment Dis	Journal of Nervous and Mental Disease (Baltimore)
J Pathol	Journal of Pathology (London)
J Psychiat Nurs	Journal of Psychiatric Nursing (Tharofare, New Jersey)
J Reprod Fertil	Journal of Reproduction and Fertitlity (Oxford)
J Roy Coll Gen Pract	Journal of the Royal College of Genera Practitioners (Dartmouth, England)
J Urban L	Journal of Urban Law (Detroit)

Jap J Midwife	Japanese Journal for Midwives (Tokyo)
Jap J Public Health Nurse	Japanese Journal of Public Health Nurse (Tokyo)
Journal of Law Reform	Journal of Law Reform (Ann Arbor)
Kango	Kango (Tokyo)
Katilolehti	Katilolehti (Helsinki)
Ky L J	Kentucky Law Journal (Lexington)
Ladies Home J	Ladies Home Journal (New York)
Lakartidningen	Lakartidningen (Stockholm)
Lancet	Lancet (London)
Life	Life (New York)
Loyola L Rev	Loyola University of Chicago Law Journal (Lincoln, Nebraska)
Manch Med Gaz or Manchester Med Gaz	Manchester Medical Gazette (Manchester)
Mayo Clin Proc	Mayo Clinic Proceedings (Rochester, Minn.)
Med Ann DC	Medical Annals of the District of Columbia (Washington)
Med J	Medical Journal (Yugoslavia)
Med J Aust	Medical Journal of Australia (Sydney)
Med Leg Bull	Medico - Legal Bulletin (Richmond)
Med Opinion & Rev	Medical Opinion and Review (New York)
Med Sestra	Meditsinskaia Sestra (Moscow)
Medicoleg J	Medico-Legal Journal (Cambridge, England)
Mental Hygiene	Mental Hygiene (New York)
Mercer L Rev	Mercer Law Review (Macon, Georgia)
Mich Med	Michigan Medicine (East Lansing)
Midwives Chron	Midwives Chronicle (London)
Milbank Memorial Fund Q	Milbank Memorial Fund Quarterly (New York)
Minerva Ginec or Minerva Ginecol	Minerva Ginecologica (Torino)
Minerva Med	Minerva Medica (Torino)
Minn L Rev	Minnesota Law Review (Minneapolis)
Minn Med	Minnesota Medicine (St. Paul)
Mlle	Madamoiselle (New York)
Mod Hosp	Modern Hospital (Chicago)
Mod Treat	Modern Treatment (New York)
Motive	Motive (Nashville, Tennessee)
Munca Sanit	Munca Sanitara (Bucharest)

Munchen Med Wschr	Muenchener Medizinische Wochenschr (Munich)
NY Times Mag	New York Times Magazine (New York)
NZ Med J	New Zealand Medical Journal (Wellington)
Nagoya Med J	Nagoya Journal of Medical Science (Nagoya)
Nat R	National Review (New York)
Nation	Nation (New York)
Natural Resources J	Natural Resources Journal (Albequerq New Mexico)
Nature	Nature (London)
Nebraska Med J	Nebraska State Medical Journal (Linc
Nebraska Nurse	Nebraska Nurse (Omaha)
Ned Tijdschr Verloskd Gynaecol	Nederlandsch Tijdschrift voor Verlo-skunde en Gynaecologie (Haarlem)
Nederl T Geneesk	Nederlands Tijdschrift voor Genee-skunde (Amsterdam)
New Eng J Med	New England Journal of Medicine (Boston)
New Repub	New Republic (Washington)
New Statesman	New Statesman (London)
Newsweek	Newsweek (New York)
New York J Med	New York State Journal of Medicine (New York)
New York Law Journal	New York Law Journal (Middletown, Connecticut)
New Zeal Nurs J	New Zealand Nursing Journal (Wellington)
Nord Med	Nordisk Medicin (Stockholm)
Northw Med	Northwest Medicine (Seattle)
Notre Dame or Notre Dame Law	Norte Dame Lawyer (Notre Dame)
Nova Scotia Med Bull	Nova Scotia Medical Bulletin (Halifax
Nurs Mirror	Nursing Mirror and Midwives Journal (London)
Obstet Gynec	Obstetrics and Gynecology (New York
Ohio Med J	Ohio State Medical Journal (Columbus
Ore L Rev	Oregon Law Review (Eugene)
Orv Hetil	Orvosi Hetilap (Budapest)
P Rico Enferm	Puerto Rico y su Enferma (Rio Piedras)

'layboy	Playboy (Chicago)
'ractitioner	Practitioner (London)
'resse Med	Presse Medicale (Paris)
'roc R Soc Med	Proceedings of the Royal Society of Medicine (London)
'sychiatr Commun	Psychiatric Communications (Pittsburgh)
sychology Today	Psychology Today (Del Mar, California)
rzegl Lek	Praeglad Lekarski (Krakow)
Med Rev	Quarterly Medical Review (Bombay)
Soc Health J	Royal Society of Health Journal (London)
JT	LaRevue Juridique Thémis (Montreal)
N	RN; National Magazine for Nurses (Oradell, New Jersey)
amp Mag or Ramparts	Ramp Magazine (Berkeley, California)
edbook	Redbook Magazine (New York)
egan Rep Nurs Law	Regan Report on Nursing Law (New York)
'eligion In Life	Religion In Life (Nashville, Tennessee)
'ev Columbia Obstet Ginec	Revista Colombiana de Obstetricia y Ginecologia (Bogota)
'ev Fr Gynecol Obstet or Rev Franc Gynec Obstet	Revue Francaise de Gynecologie et d'Obstetrique (Paris)
ev Obstet Ginecol Venez	Revista Obstetricia y Ginecologia de Venezuela (Caracas)
ipon Forum	Ripon Forum (Cambridge, Massachusetts)
A Nurs J	S. A. Nursing Journal/S. A. Verpleging- stydskrif (Pretoria, South Africa)
Afr Med J	South African Medical Journal (Capetown)
D L Rev	South Dakota Law Review (Vermillion)
TLJ	South Texas Law Journal (Houston)
aishin Igaku	Saishin Igaku (Osaka)
an Diego L Rev	San Diego Law Review (San Diego)
anfujin Jissai	Sanfujinka no Jissai (Tokyo)
anta Clara Law	Santa Clara Lawyer (Santa Clara)
at N	Saturday Night (Toronto)
ci N	Science News (Washington)
cience	Science (Washington)
cientific American	Scientific American (New York)
emin Psychiat	Seminars in Psychiatry (New York)
ocial Justice Rev	Social Justice Review (St. Louis)

Soins	Soins (Paris)
Southern Med J	Southern Medical Journal (Birmingham
Sr Schol	Senior Scholastic (New York)
Studies in Family Planning	Studies in Family Planning (New Yor】
Suffolk U L Rev	Suffolk University of Law Review (Boston)
T Norsk Laegeforen or Tidsskr Nor Laegeforen	Tidsskrift for Den Norske Laegeforen (Oslo)
T Sygepl	Tidsskrift for Sygepleje (Copenhagen】
T Ziekenverpl	Tijdschrift Voor Ziekenverpleging (Amsterdam)
Temp L Q	Temple Law Quarterly (Philadelphia)
Tex Tech L Rev	Texas Tech Law Review (Austin)
Time	Time (Chicago)
Todays Hlth	Todays Health Magazine (Chicago)
Turk Hij Tecr Biyol Derg	Turk Hijiyen ve Tecrubi Biyoloji Der【 (Ankara)
U Colo L Rev	University of Colorado Law Review (Boulder)
U Pa L Rev	University of Pennsylvania Law Revi (Philadelphia)
US News	U. S. News and World Report (Washington)
Ugeskr Laeg	Ugeskrift for Laeger (Kobenhavn)
Union Med Can	Union Medicale du Canada (Montreal)
Vand L Rev	Vanderbill Law Review (Nashville)
Vestn Oftalmol	Vestnik Oftal'mologii (Moscow)
Vestn Rentgen Radiol	Vestnik Rentgenologii I Radiologii (Moscow)
Vital Speeches	Vital Speeches (Southold, Long Islan【
Vopr Okhr Matterin Det	Voprosy Okhrany Materinstva i Detstva (Moscow)
WHO Tech Rep Ser	World Health Organization Technical Report Series (Geneva)
Wall St J	Wall Street Journal (New York)
Wash L Rev	Washington Law Review (Seattle)
Wash U L Q	Washington University Law Quarterly (St. Louis)
Washburn L J	Washburn Law Journal (Topeka, Kans
Wiad Lek	Wiadomosci Lekarskie (Warsaw)
Willamette L J	Willamette Law Journal (Salem, Oreg【
Wis L Rev	Wisconsin Law Review (Lincoln, Nebraska)

Wom Phych	Woman Physician (New York)
Woman's Day	Woman's Day (New York)
Women Law	Women Lawyer's Journal (Chicago)
Your Gov't	Your Government (Lawrence, Kansas)
Zbl Gynaek	Zentralblatt fur Gynaekologie (Leipzig)

SUBJECT HEADINGS USED IN THIS BIBLIOGRAPHY

Adoption
Abnormalities
Abortion Act
Anesthesia
Antibodies
Artificial Interruption
Behavior
Candidiasis
Cephaloridine
Cervical Incompetence or
  Insufficiency
Cesarean Section
Clinical Aspects
Complications
Contraception
Diagnosis
Drug Therapy
EACA
Ethinyl Estradiol
Family Planning
Fertility
Fertilization
Fetus
Genetics
Gynaecology
Habitual Abortion
Hemorrhage
History
Hormones
Hospitals and Abortion
Induced Abortion
Infection
IUD
Labor
Law Enforcement
Laws and Legislation
Listeriosis
Male Attitudes
Metacin

Microbiology
Menstruation
Miscarriage
Morbidity
Mortality
Mycoplasma
Nurses and Abortion
Obstetrics
Oxytocin
Periactin
Physicians and Abortions
Population
Post Abortum Complications
Potassium Permanganate
Pregnancy Interruption
Prevention and Control
Progesterone
Prostaglandins
Psychiatry
Religion
RhoGam
Sepsis
Septic Abortion
Septic Abortion and Septic
  Shock
Sexual Disorders
Sociology
Statistics
Sterility
Sterility and Sterilization
Students
Surgical Treatment and
  Management
Techniques of Abortion
Termination
Therapeutic Abortion
Transplacental Hemorrhage
Women's Liberation
Youth

TABLE OF CONTENTS

Preface i

List of Abbreviations iii

Subject Headings Used in this Bibliography xii

Books 1

Periodical Literature:

    Title Index 3

    Subject Index 45

Author Index 119

BOOKS

Callahan, Daniel. ABORTION LAW, CHOICE AND MORALITY. New York: Macmillan, 1970.

Dollen, Charles J. ABORTION IN CONTEXT: A SELECT BIBLIOGRAPHY. Metuchen, New Jersey: Scarecrow, 1970.

Committee on Psychiatry and Law and Group For The Advancement Of Psychiatry. RIGHT TO ABORTION: A PSYCHIATRIC VIEW. New York: Charles Scribner's & Sons, 1970.

David, Henry P. FAMILY PLANNING AND ABORTION IN THE SOCIALIST COUNTRIES OF CENTRAL AND EASTERN EUROPE. Bridgeport, Connecticut: Key Book Service, 1970.

Ebon, Martin, editor. EVERY WOMAN'S GUIDE TO ABORTION. New York: Universe Books, 1970.

Freeman, Lucy, editor. DR. X. ABORTIONIST. New York: Grove Press, 1970.

Glass, Robert H. and Nathan G. Kase. WOMAN'S CHOICE: A GUIDE TO CONTRACEPTION, FERTILITY, ABORTION, AND MENOPAUSE. New York: Basic Books, 1970.

Grisez, Germain. ABORTION: THE MYTHS, THE REALITIES, AND THE ARGUMENTS. New York: World Publishing Company, 1970.

Hall, Robert E., editor. ABORTION IN A CHANGING WORLD. 2 Volumes. New York: Columbia University Press, 1970.

Kitwood, T. M. WHAT IS HUMAN. Downer's Grove, Illinois: Inter-Varsity, 1970.

McCarthy, John F. IN DEFENSE OF HUMAN LIFE. Houston, Texas: Lumen Christi Press, 1970.

New Jersey. Committee to study the New Jersey statutes relating to abortion. FINAL REPORT TO THE LEGISLATURE, DECEMBER 31, 1969. Trenton, New Jersey: The Committee, 1970.

New Jersey. General Assembly. Judiciary Committee. PUBLIC HEARING ON ASSEMBLY BILL NO. 762, HELD, TRENTON NEW JERSEY, APRIL 9, 1970. Trenton, New Jersey: The Committee, 1970.

Noonan, John T., Jr., editor. MORALITY OF ABORTION: LEGAL AND HISTORICAL PERSPECTIVES. Cambridge: Harvard University Press, 1970.

O'Neil, Daniel J. CHURCH LOBBYING IN A WESTERN STATE: A CASE STUDY ON ABORTION LEGISLATION (Arizona Government Studies, No. 7). Tucson, Arizona: University of Arizona Press, 1970.

Rusinow, Dennison I. POPULATION REVIEW 1970: YUGOSLAVIA (Fieldstaff Reports: Southeast Europe Series, V. 17, No. 1). Hanover, New Hampshire: American Universities Fieldstaff, 1970.

Society of Friends. American Friends Service Committee. WHO SHALL LIVE? MAN'S CONTROL OVER BIRTH AND DEATH; A REPORT. New York: Hill & Wang, 1970.

Washington State. ACT RELATING TO ABORTION (Ch. 3, Session Laws, 1970). Olympia, Washington: State of Washington, 1970.

PERIODICAL LITERATURE

TITLE INDEX

"Aberrant karyotypes and spontaneous abortion in a Japanese family,"
by T. Kadotani, et al. NATURE (London) 225:735-737, February 21, 1970.

"Abnormalities of early human development," by B. F. Stratford.
AMER J OBSTET GYNEC 107:1223-1232, August 15, 1970.

"Abortion," AJN 70:1919, September, 1970.

"Abortion," NAT R 22:658-659, June 30, 1970.

"Abortion," NOVA SCOTIA MED BULL 49:34, April, 1970.

"Abortion," by C. J. Enschede. NEDERL T GENEESK 114:1219-
1221, July 18, 1970.

"Abortion," by C. Heine. CANAD MED ASS J 102:1211, May 30, 1970.

"Abortion," by R. LeRoux, et al. AMER J NURS 70:1919-1925,
September, 1970.

"Abortion," by H. Morgentaler. CANAD MED ASS J 102:876, April,
1970.

"Abortion. Condescension or prevention," by R. S. Wurm. MED J AUST
1:557-562, March 14, 1970.

"Abortion. Should the physician be the conscience of society?" by
E. B. Linton, et al. OBSTET GYNEC 35:465-467, March, 1970.

"Abortion: the academic angle," MLLE 72:145, December, 1970.

3

"Abortion act," by J. P. Crawford. LANCET 2:1138, November 28, 1970.

"The abortion act: a general practitioner's view," by J. McEwan. PRACTITIONER 204:427-432, March, 1970.

"Abortion act in action," by C. B. Goodhart. NATURE (London) 227: 757-758, August 15, 1970.

"The Abortion Act 1967. (a). The advantages and disadvantages," by D. Baird. R SOC HEALTH J 90:291-295, November-December, 1970.

"The Abortion Act (1967). Findings of an inquiry into the first year's working of the Act conducted by the Royal College of Obstetricians and Gynaecologists," BRIT MED J 2:529-535, May 30, 1970.

"Abortion analysis," by P. Diggory. LANCET 2:413-414, August 22, 1970.

"Abortion and adoption," by C. Schoenberg. CHILD WELFARE 49:544, December, 1970.

"Abortion and the birth rate in the USSR," by G. Hyde. J BIOSOC SCI 2:283-292, July, 1970.

"Abortion and catecholamines," by T. K. Eskes. NED TIJDSCHR VERLOSKD GYNAECOL 70:465-474, October, 1970.

"Abortion and the changing law," NEWSWEEK 75:53-56+, April 13, 1970.

"Abortion and the constitutional question," SD L REV 15:318, Spring, 1970.

"Abortion and the courts," SCIENTIFIC AMERICAN 222:50+, January, 1970.

"Abortion and genetic disorders," by V. G. Kirkels. NED TIJDSCHR VERLOSKD GYNAECOL 70:445-453, October, 1970.

"Abortion and the hospital," by P. A. Richardson, et al. NEW YORK J MED 70:2144-2145, August 15, 1970.

4

"Abortion and the just society," by N. F. Isaacs. RJT 5:27, 1970.

"Abortion and the law: anachronisms racing science," J MISSISSIPPI MED ASS 11:335-336, June, 1970.

"Abortion and legal rationality," by J. Finnis. ADELAIDE L REV 3: 431, August, 1970.

"Abortion and responsibility," AMERICA 122:400, April 18, 1970.

"Abortion and sterilization. Status of the law in mid-1970," by N. Hershey. AMER J NURS 70:1926-1927, September, 1970.

"Abortion and suicidal behaviors: observations on the concept of endangering the mental health of the mother," by H. L. P. Resnik, et al. MENTAL HYGIENE 55:10-20, January, 1970.

"Abortion and the unwanted child (United States): an interview with Alan F. Guttmacher, M.D. and Harriet F. Pilpel," FAMILY PLANNING PERSPECTIVES 2:16-24, March, 1970.

"Abortion attitudes of poverty level blacks," by C. E. Vincent, et al. SEMIN PSYCHIAT 2,3:309-317, 1970.

"Abortion capital," by C. B. Goodhart. LANCET 1:367, February 14, 1970.

"Abortion caravan," by K. Maeots, CAN FORUM 50:157, July-August, 1970.

"Abortion: The Catholic viewpoint," by F. J. Ayd, Jr. SEMIN PSYCHIAT 2,3:258-262, 1970.

"Abortion caused by type II Herpesvirus. Isolation of the virus from cultures of zygotic tissues," by A. Boué, et al. PRESSE MED 78: 103-106, January 17, 1970.

"Abortion comes out of the shadows," LIFE 68:20B, February 27, 1970.

"Abortion: condescension or prevention," by B. McKie. MED J AUST 1:821, April 18, 1970.

"Abortion-constitutional law-a law that allows an abortion only when "necessary to preserve" the life of the mother violates a qualified constitutional right to an abortion and is unconstitutionally vague,"

5

TEX L REV 48:937, May, 1970.

"Abortion counseling in legal trouble: Rabbi Ticktin on conspiracy charges," CHR CENT 87:68, January 21, 1970.

"Abortion: crime or privilege?" by J. M. Hannaford. MAYO CLIN PROC 45:510-516, July, 1970.

"Abortion debate," COMMONWEAL 92:131-132, April 24, 1970.

X "Abortion dogmas needing research scrutiny," by E. Pohlman. SEMIN PSYCHIAT 2,3:220-230, 1970.

"Abortion: due process and the doctor's dilemma," J FAMILY L 9:300, 1970.

"Abortion goes public. Hospitals report 2,000 abortions in first week under new N.Y. law," MOD HOSP 115:33-36, August, 1970.

"Abortion, the hospital and the law," by D. F. Phillips. HOSPITALS 44:59-62, August, 1970.

"Abortion in America," by H. Rosen. AMER J PSYCHIAT 126:1299-1301, March, 1970.

"Abortion in court," ECONOMIST 234:48, February 28, 1970.

"Abortion in the first trimester. Anatomico-clinical studies of 100 cases," by Esquivel A. Cerón, et al. GINECOL OBSTET MEX 28: 449-461, October, 1970.

"Abortion in New York," NEWSWEEK 76:52, October 5, 1970.

"Abortion in New York," TIME 96:48, September 7, 1970.

"Abortion incorporated," JAMA 214:362, October, 1970.

"Abortion is no man's business," by N. Shainess. PSYCHOLOGY TODAY 3:18-24, May, 1970.

X "Abortion is the world's most common (and worst) population regulator," by G. Machanik. SA NURS J 36:32-33 passim, April, 1970.

"The abortion issue," by H. Teilmann. T SYGEPL 70:10-11, January, 1970.

"Abortion Law," NEW STATESMAN 80:138, August 7, 1970.

"Abortion Law," NEW STATESMAN 80:786, December 11, 1970.

"Abortion law-California abortion law voided," DICK L REV 74:772, Summer, 1970.

"Abortion: law, ethics and the value of life," by C. Burke. MANCH MED GAZ 49:4-9, July, 1970.

"Abortion law in Massachusetts," by M. L. Taymor. NEW ENG J MED 283:602, September 10, 1970.

"Abortion law reform," by L. R. Worsnop. EDITORIAL RESEARCH REPTS p. 545-562, July 24, 1970.

"Abortion law reform: how the controversy changed," by M. Simms. CRIM L R 1970:567, October, 1970.

"Abortion law reform progress in Michigan," by J. M. Stack. MICH MED 69:23-27, January, 1970.

"Abortion laws: an appeal for repeal (proposes repeal (not reform) of all laws relating to abortion except those governing the practice of medicine generally)," by G. Clyde Dodder. RIPON FORUM 6:20-22, May, 1970.

"Abortion laws: a commentary," by Neil Snortland. YOUR GOVT 25: 3-4, March 15, 1970.

"Abortion laws. Constitutional questions," by A. R. Holder. JAMA 214:2405-2406, December 28, 1970.

"Abortion laws: a study in social change," by T. G. Moyers. SAN DIEGO L REV 7:237, May, 1970.

"Abortion laws, under challenge, are being liberalized (United States)," CONG Q W REPT 28:1913-1916, July 24, 1970.

"Abortion: a legal view," by N. W. Williamson. NZ MED J 72:257-261, October, 1970.

"Abortion legislation: a fundamental challenge," by L. Massett. SCI N 97:75-76, January 17, 1970.

"Abortion lib.," by J. Dingman. CHATELAINE 43:4, July, 1970.

"Abortion: the lonely problem," RN 33:34-39, June, 1970.

"Abortion made easier," CHR TODAY 14:36, March 27, 1970.

"Abortion: The medical and psychological view," by J. E. Brody. WOMAN'S DAY 34:68+, October, 1970.

"Abortion: new and old issues," AMERICA 122:666-667, June 27, 1970

"Abortion: the new civil right," by E. Truninger. WOMEN LAW 56:86, Summer, 1970.

X "Abortion: new studies," COMMONWEAL 93:76-77, October 16, 1970.

"Abortion on demand," by J. A. Fitzgerald. MED OPINION & REV 6: 110+, January, 1970.

"Abortion on demand: New York and Hawaii," TIME 96:34, July 6, 197

X "Abortion-on-demand: whose morality?" by R. M. Byrn. NOTRE DAME LAW 46:5, Fall, 1970.

"Abortion on request: Hawaii," TIME 95:34, March 9, 1970.

"Abortion on request: Its consequences for population trends and public health," by C. Tietze. SEMIN PSYCHIAT 2,3:375-381, 1970.

"Abortion or no? What decides? An inquiry by questionnaire into the attitudes of gynecologists and psychiatrists in Aberdeen," by C. McCance, et al. SEMIN PSYCHIAT 2,3:352-360, 1970.

"Abortion, Oregon style," ORE L REV 49:302, April, 1970.

"Abortion: a physician's view," by W. R. Roy. WASHBURN L J 9:391, Spring, 1970.

"Abortion reform," TIME 95:46, April 20, 1970.

"Abortion reform: history, status, and prognosis," W. Case. RES L REV 21:521, April, 1970.

"Abortion reform: the new tokenism," by L. Cisler. RAMPARTS 9:19-25, August, 1970.

'Abortion request and post operative response. A Washington Community Survey," by R. J. Pion, et al. NORTHW MED 69:693-698. 1970.

'The abortion revolution," by R. Hall, M.D. PLAYBOY 17:112-114+, September, 1970.

'Abortion: a startling proposal," by M. J. Halberstam. REDBOOK 134: 78-79+, April, 1970.

'Abortion--a stormy subject," RN 33:53-69, September, 1970.

'The abortion survey," by J. L. Moore, Jr. J MED ASSOC GA 59:459-460, December, 1970.

Abortion: a theologian's view," by P. R. Ramsey. AORN J 12:55-62, November, 1970.

'Abortion tumult," SR SCHOL 96:7-8, May 4, 1970.

Abortion under the new Colorado law," by S. W. Downing et al. NEBRASKA MED J 55:24-30, January, 1970.

Abortion unlimited," NEWSWEEK 75:46, March 9, 1970.

Abortion veto: legislation vetoed by Maryland's Governor Marvin Mandel," NEW REPUB 162:8, June 13, 1970.

Abortion--where do we go from here?" by D. Cashman. CATH NURSE 32:22-27, March, 1970.

Abortion without surgery? using prostaglandin F2 alpha," TIME 95: 39-40, February 9, 1970.

Abortion: yes or no?" by R. B. Zachary. MANCH MED GAZ 50:4-5, October, 1970.

Abortions: change of heart," NATURE (London) 227:11, July 4, 1970.

Abortions on demand," NEWSWEEK 76:60, July 13, 1970.

Abortions under the N.H.S.," by H. G. Arthure. BR MED J 4:617, December 5, 1970.

"Abortus provocatus, ethics and legislation," by A. Strom. T NORSK LAEGEFOREN 90:685-687, April 1, 1970.

"About abortion," JAMA 215:286, January 11, 1971.

"Absence of antidiuresis during administration of prostaglandin F2 alpha," by G. Roberts et al. BRIT MED J 2:152-154, April 18, 1970

"Action of privy Council on appeals from G.M.C." BRIT MED J 1:292 August 1, 1970.

"Administration of epsilon-aminocaproic acid (EACA) in the prevention of fibrinolytic hemorrhages associated with the expulsion of the fetus remaining in the uterus after its death," by E. Howorka, et al WIAD LEK 23:973-977, June, 1970.

"After abortion reform," AMERICA 122:449, April 25, 1970.

"After July 1, an abortion should be as simple to have as a tonsillecto my, but--," by L. Greenhouse. N Y TIMES MAG p. 7+, June 28, 197

"Aging of fertilizing gametes and spontaneous abortion. Effect of the day of ovulation and the time of insemination," by R. Guerrero, et al. AMER J OBSTET GYNEC 107:263-267, May 15, 1970.

"Analysis of blood loss in artificial termination of pregnancy under local anesthesia," by J. Higier, et al. WIAD LEK 23:1289-1293, August 1, 1970.

"Anatomic and chromosomal anomalies in spontaneous abortion. Possi ble correlation with overripeness of oocytes," by K. Mikamo. AME J OBSTET GYNEC 106:243-254, January 15, 1970.

"Another opinion on abortion," by D. Conry. NEBRASKA NURSE 3:9- 10, May, 1970.

"Anti-abortion lobby: Catholic resistance to New York state's bill," by J. Deedy. COMMONWEAL 92:154, May 1, 1970. Discussion 92:255, May 22, 1970.

"Apropos of embryotoxic and teratogenic actions of "triton W.R. 1339" in the mouse: influence of vitamin A," by C. Roussel, et al. C R ACAD SCI (D) 271:215-218, July 15, 1970.

Are state abortion statutes reasonable?--The recent judicial trend indicates the contrary," S T L J 11:426, 1970.

Artificial pregnancy interruption and birth rate," by K. Vácha. CESK GYNEK 35:329-320, July, 1970.

Assessment of the obstetric application of 17-hydroxyprogesterone capronate (Hormofort)," by S. Németi, et al. ORV HETIL 111:1404-1407, June 14, 1970.

Association of maternal genital herpetic infection with spontaneous abortion," by Z. M. Naib, et al. OBSTET GYNEC 35:260-263, February, 1970.

Atonic hemorrhage in pregnancy interruption and its complications due to coagulation disorders," by O. Vago.ZBL GYNAEK 92:62-63, January 10, 1970.

Attempted prevention of the embryotoxic and teratogenic effects of actinomycin D. II. Influence of the lactogenic hormone," by H. Tuchmann-Duplessis, et al. C R SOC BIOL 164:60-63, 1970.

Background of a lost baby," by B. J. Hughes. NURS MIRROR 131:46-48, October 23, 1970.

Bacteremia shock syndrome in obstetrics," by I. Szemesi, et al. ACTA CHIR SCI HUNG 11:87-95, 1970.

Benzidamine and tetracycline therapy in gynecologic and obstetrical pathology," by L. Tinelli, et al. MINERVA GINECOL 22:677-680, July 15, 1970.

Birth control and abortions legal battles past and present. Summary of paper given at annual meeting November 5-8, 1969," by H. Pilpel. WOM PHYCH 25,7:435-436, 1970.

Blood circulation and temperature of the uterus in a normal pregnancy and in threatened premature labor," by T. A. Serova, et al. VOPR OKHR MATERIN DET 15:71-74, November, 1970.

Britain's abortion act: inquiry requested," by T. Beeson. CHR CENT 87:984-985, August 19, 1970.

A case against abortion: plea for the unborn child," by M. A. Duffy.

11

NEW YORK LAW JOURNAL 164:1+, September 23, 1970; also in WOMEN LAW 56:86, Summer, 1970.

"A case for abortion and unrestrictive laws," by B. E. Fisher. THE N YORK LAW JOURNAL 164:1+, September 24, 1970; also in WOME LAW 56:86, Summer, 1970.

"A case of bacteremic shock with acute pulmonar edema during aborti by F. Charvet, et al. BULL FED GYNEC OBSTET FRANC 22:67 January-March, 1970.

"A case of encephalocele in a fetus in pregnancy complicated by imminent abortion," by A. Lipinski, et al. WIAD LEK 23:1239-1241, July 15, 1970.

"Catholics and abortion," by W. F. Buckley jr.," NAT R 22:1366-13(December 15, 1970.

"Cause of action for "wrongful life": a suggested analysis," MINN L REV 55:58, November, 1970.

"Cephaloridine in septic abortion. Comparison with a conventional combined antibiotic regimen in a conservative program of management," by W. E. Josey, et al. AMER J OBSTET GYNEC 106:237-242, January 15, 1970.

"Certain indices of glucocorticold function of the adrenal cortex in postabortion sepsis," by M. G. Simakova. AKUSH GINEKOL 46:1 18, February, 1970.

"Certification of rape under the Colorado abortion statute," U COLO] REV 42:121, May, 1970.

"Cervical incompetence in multiple pregnancy," by G. W. McGowan. OBSTET GYNEC 35:589-591, April, 1970.

"Cervical insufficiency," by O. Hirokawa. SAISHIN IGAKU 25:671-6 March, 1970.

"Cervical insufficiency in pregnancy. McDonald's surgical method,"] P. Rössner. DTSCH GESUNDHEITSW 25:750-754, April, 1970.

"Change the abortion law now; editorial," by D. Anderson. CHATEL/ 43:1, September, 1970.

'Christian choices in a liberal abortion climate," by R. F. R. Gardner. CHR TODAY 14:6-8, May 22, 1970.

'Chromosomal abnormalities and spontaneous abortion," MED J AUST 2:992-994, November 28, 1970.

'Chromosomal anomalies in spontaneously aborted human fetuses," by R. K. Dhadial, et al. LANCET 2:20-21, July 4, 1970.

'Chromosome aberrations in human spontaneous abortion," by J. G. Boué, et al. PRESSE MED 78:635-641, March, 1970.

'Chromosome aberrations in spontaneous abortion," by P. Dráč, et al. CESK GYNEK 35:230-233, May, 1970 (42 ref.).

'Chromosome pathology in repeated abortions," by S. Rugiati, et al. MINERVA GINEC 22:81-86, January 31, 1970.

'Chromosome studies in selected spontaneous abortions. 1. Conception after oral contraceptives," by D. H. Carr. CANAD MED ASS J 103: 343-348, August 15, 1970.

'Chromosomes and abortions," by S. L. Larson, et al. MAYO CLIN PROC 45:60-72, January, 1970 (65 ref.).

'Chromosomes in spontaneous abortions," by B. Padeh, et al. HAREFUAH 78:158-161, February 15, 1970.

'Civil status and risks of abortion, premature childbirth and perinatal death," by F. Pettersson. LAKARTIDNINGEN 67:3369-3372, July 22, 1970.

'Clinical and x-ray aspects of pulmonary edema in patients with sepsis following abortion," by Kh. A. Khidirbeil, et al. VESTN RENTGEN RADIOL 45:77-82, March-April, 1970.

'Clinical aspects of hormonal protection during pregnancy," by G. A. Hauser. NED TIJDSCHR VERLOSKD GYNAECOL 70:436-445, October, 1970.

'Clinical use of depressing agents," by J. S. Skjaeraasen. TIDSSKR NOR LAEGEFOREN 90:2192-2196, December 1, 1970.

"Clinical use of prostaglandins," BR MED J 4:253-254, October 3, 1970.

"Clostridial organisms in septic abortions. Report of 7 cases," by R. O'Neill, et al. OBSTET GYNEC 35:458-461, March, 1970.

"College policy on abortion and sterilization," ACOG NURSES BULL 4:2, Fall, 1970.

"College students' attitudes toward abortion," by J. W. Maxwell. FAM COORDINATOR 19,3:247-252, July, 1970.

"The Colorado report," by A. Heller, et al. SEMIN PSYCHIAT 2,3:361 374, 1970.

"Colorado's abortion law: an obstetrician's view," by C. Dafoe. NEBRASKA MED J 55:3-4, January, 1970.

"Come and go" aspiration abortion," by A. J. Margolis. CALIF MED 113:43, December, 1970.

"Comparative epidemiologic study between patients with and without previous illegal abortions," by F. J. Aguirre Zozaya, et al. GINEC OBSTET MEX 27:147-182, February, 1970.

"Comparison of two antibiotic regimens in the treatment of septic abor tion," by D. R. Ostergard. OBSTET GYNEC 36:473-474, September 1970.

"Complication of hysterotomy," by S. V. Sood. BR MED J 4:495-496, November, 1970.

"Complications in the interruption of abortion, depending on the metho used--classical or aspiration method," by A. Atanasov. AKUSH GINEKOL (Sofiia) 9:271-277, 1970.

"Consent to continued pregnancy," by R. Matz. N ENGL J MED 283: 1522-1523, December 31, 1970.

"The consequences of criminal abortion on the woman's state of healt by M. Handru. MUNCA SANIT 18:345-348, June, 1970.

"Constitutional law-abortion-does a woman have a constitutional right under the ninth amendment to choose whether to bear a child after conception," TEX TECH L REV 2:99, Fall, 1970.

"Constitutional law-abortion-1850 California statute prohibiting all abortions not "necessary to preserve (the mother's) life" is unconstitutionally vague and an improper infringemnet on women's constitutional rights," NOTRE DAME LAW 45:329, Winter, 1970.

"Constitutional law-abortion-standard excepting abortions done as "necessary for the preservation of the mother's life or health" held unconstitutionally vague," VAND L REV 23:821, May, 1970.

"Constitutional law-abortion-statute prohibiting abortion of unquickened fetus violates mother's constitutional right of privacy," VAND L REV 23:1346, November, 1970.

"Constitutional law-crimmal abortion-statute prohibiting intentional destruction of unquickened fetus violates mother's right of privacy," GA L REV 4:907, Summer, 1970.

"Constitutional law-criminal law-requirement of certainty in legislation in a criminal abortion statute," J URBAN L 47:901, 1969-1970.

"Constitutional law-state regulation of abortion," WIS L REV 1970:933, 1970.

"Constitutional law--void-for-vagueness," SUFFOLK U L REV 4:920, Spring, 1970.

"Constitutional question: is there a right to abortion?" by L. J. Greenhouse. N Y TIMES MAG p. 30-31+, January 25, 1970; Discussion p. 14+, February 22, 1970.

"Constitutional reflections on abortion reform," by P. L. Baude. JOURNAL OF LAW REFORM 4:1-10, Fall, 1970.

Consultants' report on abortion," BRIT MED J 2:491-492, May 30, 1970.

Contraception and abortion: American Catholic responses," by D. Callahan. AMERICAN ACADEMY OF POLITICAL AND SOCIAL SCIENCE. ANNALS. 387:109-117, February, 1970.

Control of fertility," by M. L. Peterson. NEW ENG J MED 282:1432-1433, June 18, 1970.

"Counseling and referral for legal abortion in California's (San Francisco) bay area," by Sadja Goldsmith, et al. FAMILY PLANNING PERSPECTIVES 2:14-19, June, 1970.

"Course and outcome of labor after threatened abortion," by H. Wallner et al. GEBURTSHILFE FRAUENHEILKD 30:504-513, June, 1970.

"Crime of abortion; address, April 9, 1970," by B. F. Brown. VITAL SPEECHES 36:549-553, July 1, 1970.

"Criminal law-abortion-man, being without a legal beginning," KY L J 58:843, Summer, 1969-1970.

"Criminal law-abortion statute-due process-the supreme court of California has held that a statute prohibiting abortions not "necessary ⟨ preserve" the mother's life is so vague and uncertain as to be viola tive to the fourteenth amendment's due process clause," DUQUESN L REV 8:439, Summer, 1970.

"Criminal procedure-search and seizure-electronic eavesdropping-abortion: recording of voluntary conversation between police agent and defendant admissible in evidence," WASH L REV 45:411, April, 1970.

"Critical study of mono and diphasic methods of artificial interruption of pregnancy," by W. Weise, et al. ZBL GYNAK 92,26:841-848, 19⟨

"The culture of poverty in relation to disease in Latin America," by L. S. Miranda. P RICO ENFERM 45:14-15 concl, March, 1970.

"Current status of abortion and premature births in cities," KANGO 2⟨ 117-122, May, 1970.

"Cytogenetic aspects of habitual abortion. 2. Observation of satellite association in couples with history of habitual abortion," by K. Koike. NAGOYA MED J 16:72-79, November, 1970.

"Cytogenetic studies on mid-trimester abortuses," by P. Ruzicska, et al. HUMANGENETIK 10:273-297, 1970.

"Cytogenetics of spontaneous abortion. The chromosomes of decidua,' by D. T. Arakaki, et al. AMER J OBSTET GYNEC 107:1199-1204, August 15, 1970.

"Data of value in the prognosis of threatened abortion," by V. Ruiz Velasco, et al. REV OBSTET GINECOL VENEZ 30:109-124, 1970.

"Death following criminal abortion with hypertonic saline," by G. Weiss. NEW YORK J MED 70:312-315, January 15, 1970.

"Debates on abortion in United States," PRESSE MED 78:1899-1900, October 17, 1970.

"The Declaration of Oslo," S AFR MED J 44:1281, November 14, 1970.

"Definitive treatment for incompetent cervix," by G. P. Charlewood. S AFR MED J 44:1367-1368, November 28, 1970.

"The dermal graft and cervical incompetency," by J. L. Breen. INT J FERTIL 15:1-13, January-March, 1970.

"Determinant factors in habitual abortion," by C. MacGregor, et al. GINEC OBSTET MEX 27:331-350, March, 1970.

"Diagnostic error while using ultrasonic diagnosis in the question: extrauterine pregnancy or abortus imminens," by W. Nusch. GEBURTSHILFE FRAUENHEILKD 30:1120-1122, December, 1970.

"Differences in the submicroscopic structure of the epithelial cells of the secreting endometrium in healthy women and women with habitual abortions," by M. Dvořák, et al. ZENTRALBL GYNAEKOL 92: 1241-1248, September 19, 1970.

'Earth Day revisited," by A. Savage. IMPRINT 17:8, September-October, 1970.

'Easier abortion," SCI AM 222:47-48, June, 1970.

'Editorial," CANAD NURSE 66:3, November, 1970.

'Effect of gestational and maternal age in early abortion," by D. T. Arakaki, et al. OBSTET GYNEC 35:264-269, February, 1970.

'Effect of induced abortion on birth rate: a simulation model," by S. Mukherji, et al. INDIAN J PUBLIC HEALTH 14:49-58, January, 1970.

'The effect of oxytocin on the complication rate of early therapeutic abortions, " by E. D. B. Johansson. AETA OBSTET GYNEC SCAND

49,2:129-131, 1970.

"Effect of prostaglandins on human uterus in pregnancy," by M. P. Embrey. J REPROD FERTIL 23:372-373, November, 1970.

"Effective surgical procedures for interruption of pregnancy in the second trimester," by Y. Onishi. SANFUJIN JISSAI 19:73-78, January, 1970.

"The effects of anesthesia and pulmonary ventilation on blood loss during elective therapeutic abortion," by B. F. Cullen, et al. ANES THESIOLOGY 32:108-113, February, 1970.

"Effects of anesthesia in therapeutic abortion," by W. H. Forrest Jr. ANESTHESIOLOGY 33:121-122, July, 1970.

"Endometrium and the sequelae of abortion," by E. Philippe, et al. REV FRANC GYNEC OBSTET 65:413-421, July-august, 1970.

"Endonasal electrophoresis in the treatment of premature labor," by V. I. Bodiazhina, et al. AKUSH GINEK 46:58-65, April, 1970.

"Estrogenic insufficiency and genetic abortions," by J. Cohen, et al. BULL FED SOC GYNECOL OBSTET LANG FR 22:439-442, September-October, 1970.

"The ethics of abortion," by C. W. Sem-Jacobsen, et al. AMER J PSYCHIAT 127:536-538, October, 1970.

"Evaluation of the effectiveness of metacin therapy in threatened premature labor and late abortion (clinico-hysterographic study)," by M. Ia. Martynshin. AKUSH GINEK 46:39-43, January, 1970.

"Evaluation of results of surgical treatment of cervical isthmus insuffi ciency being the cause of late abortions and miscarriages," by W. Kokoszka, et al. PRZEGL LEK 26:769-770, 1970.

"Evaluation of sequellae and possibilities of pregnancy interruption by women who experienced it," by E. Dlhoš, et al. CESK GYNEK 35 336-338, July, 1970.

"Evaluation of therapeutic abortion as an element of preventive psych atry," by H. G. Whittington. AMER J PSYCHIAT 126:1224-1229, March, 1970.

"Execution without trial," by A. W. Liley. NZ NURS J 63:6-7, December, 1970.

"Experience at Duke Medical Center after modern legislation for therapeutic abortion," by A. C. Christakos. SOUTHERN MED J 63:655-657, June, 1970.

"Experience in anesthesia for artificial interrupting of pregnancy by a new intravenous anesthetic, propanidid (Epontol)," by K. Nagauchi, et al. SANFUJIN JISSAI 19:873-876, August, 1970.

"Extended birth control: Abortion on request," by J. G. Howells. CAN MENT HLTH 18:3+, September-October, 1970

"Failure of large doses of ethinyl estradiol to interfere with early embryonic development in the human species," by M. Bačič, et al. AMER J BOSTET GYNEC 107:531-534, June 15, 1970.

"Failure to advise: a basis for malpractice under the revised Oregon abortion act," WILLAMETTE L J 6:349, June, 1970.

"Failures of cervix uteri cerclage due to a fault of technic," by M. Dumont, et al. BULL FED SOC GYNECOL OBSTET LANG FR 22: 473, September-October, 1970.

"Family planning counselling," by E. F. Daily. BRIT MED J 3:345-346, August 8, 1970.

"Fathers and sons; liberalization of New York state law," NEWSWEEK 75:77, April 20, 1970.

"Fertility control: health and educational factors for the 1970s. Contraception or abortion?" by J. H. Hughes. J BIOSOC SCI 2:161-166, April, 1970.

"Fetal erythrocytes in maternal circulation after spontaneous abortion," by O. Litwak, et al. JAMA 214:531-534, October 19, 1970.

"Fetal indications for termination of pregnancy," by H. L. Nadler. SEMIN PSYCHIAT 2,3:302-308, 1970.

"Feticide infanticide upon request," by P. Ramsey. RELIGION IN LIFE 39:170-186, Summer, 1970.

"Feto-maternal haemorrhage at therapeutic abortion," by A. H. John, et al. J OBSTET GYNAEC BRIT COMM 77:137-138, February, 1970

"Fetuses and newborns of 95 per cent pancreatectomized female rats," by V. G. Foglia. ADVANCES METAB DIS 1:Suppl 1:221+, 1970.

"1st liberalization of the abortion legislation in USA," by J. Padovec. CESK GYNEK 35:381, July, 1970.

"The foetus began to cry...abortion. 1." by G. H. Green. NEW ZEAL NURS J 63:11-12, July, 1970; 2. 63:6-7, August, 1970; 3. 63:11-12, September, 1970.

"Foreign body in the abdominal cavity," by A. Murdzhiev, et al. AKUSH GINEKOL (Sofiia) 9:347-348, 1970.

"Foreign body in urinary bladder from attempted abortion," by G. S. Bernstein, et al. OBSTET GYNEC 36:475-478, September, 1970.

"The formation of bone in uterine tissues," by A. Springer, et al. REV FRANC GYNEC OBSTET 65:519-522, September, 1970.

"Fracture of curette," by J. M. McGarry. BRIT MED J 1:49, January 3, 1970.

"Free abortion," by L. Valvanne. KATILOLEHTI 75:91, March, 1970.

"Freedom in family planning. The abortion law and women's liberation," by H. Muramatsu. JAP J MIDWIFE 24:10-19, December, 1970.

"Further course of gestation in women treated because of threatened abortion. Evaluation through vaginal smears," by R. Wawryk, et al. GINEK POL 41:395-400, April, 1970.

"Future perspectives of prenatal pediatrics," by C. Haffter. ACTA PAEDOPSYCHIATR 37:241-243, December, 1970.

"Gaines v. Wolcott (Ga) 167 S E 2d 366," MERCER L REV 21:325, Winter, 1970.

"General practitioners' views on pregnancy termination," by W. Sussma et al. MED J AUST 2:169-173, July 25, 1970.

"Georgia Abortion Law unconstitutional," by J. L. Moore Jr.," J MED

ASSOC GA 59:402-407, October, 1970.

"Guidelines for action about the New York abortion law," SOCIAL JUSTICE REVIEW 63:266-273, December, 1970.

"Gynaecology in a permissive society," by T. L. Lewis. AUST NZ J OBSTET GYNAECOL 10:244-251, November, 1970.

"The gynecologist and therapeutic abortion: the changing times," by R. R. DeAluarez, et al. SEMIN PSYCHIAT 2,3:275-282, 1970.

"Habitual abortion," by I. S. Rozovskii. MED SESTRA 29:29-32, February, 1970.

"Habitual abortion and premature labor caused by primary cervical insufficiency. Surgical and pharmacological treatment," by G. Colucci, et al. MINERVA GINECOL 21:687-688, May 31, 1969.

"Happier birthdays; the story of the National Birthday Trust," by J. Barnes. MIDWIVES CHRON 83:406-411, December, 1970.

"Hazards of 1st pregnancy interruptions," by L. Sokolik, et al. CESK GYNEK 35:373-374, July, 1970.

"Health insurance for abortion costs: a survey," by C. F. Muller. FAMILY PLANNING PERSPECTIVES 2:12-20, October, 1970.

"High doses of progesterone in the therapy of hormonal abortion and in the prevention of various types of pregnancy interruption," by C. Morra, et al. MINERVA GINECOL 21:699-701, May 31, 1969.

"High-risk obstetrics. 3. Cytohormonal evaluations and their practical utility in managing high-risk patients," by R. H. Aubry, et al. AMER J OBSTET GYNEC 107:48-64, May 1, 1970.

"Hormonal and vaginal cytology changes induced by a pregnane in threatened abortion," by J. Bravo Sandoval, et al. GINECOL OBSTET MEX 28:573-579, November, 1970.

"Hormonal problems of threatened early pregnancy," by M. Tausk. NED TIJDSCHR VERLOSKD GYNAECOL 70:430-436, October, 1970.

"Hormone levels in threatened abortion," by J. B. Brown, et al. J OBSTET GYNAEC BRIT COMM 77:690-700, August, 1970.

21

"Hospital abortion committee as an administrative body of the state," J FAMILY L 10:32, 1970.

"Follow-up of patients referred for termination of pregnancy," by C. M. Pare, et al. LANCET 1:635-638, March 28, 1970.

"How doctors perform abortions," by D. R. Zimmerman. LADIES HOME J 87:38+, November, 1970.

"How men feel about abortion," by C. Karpel MLLE 71:142-143+, June 1970.

"How to perform abortion in the 2d trimester," by J. Presl. CESK GYNEKOL 35:437-438, September, 1970.

"Human rights - What of the unborn," NEW ZEALAND NURS J 63:4, July, 1970.

"Hypertonic saline induction of abortion," by R. C. Goodlin. JAMA 211:1544, March, 1970.

"Hysterographic changes following uterine injury during artificial interruption of pregnancy," by V. Nesit. CESK GYNEK 35:353-354, July 1970.

"Hysterography in intrauterine pregnancy and abortion. Report of three cases," by M. Honoré. ACTA RADIOL (Diagn) 10:489-493, November 1970.

"The gysterosalpingographic picture following interruption of the 1st pregnancy," by L. Láska, et al. CESK GYNEK 35:352-353, July, 1970.

"Ideal means of fertility control?" by A. Gillespie, et al. LANCET 1: 717, April 4, 1970.

"I'm married, happy, and went through hell for a legal abortion," by R. Squire. PORT MACL MAG 83:51-52, 54-56, October, 1970.

"The immediate morbidity of therapeutic abortion," by M. A. Carlton, et al. MED J AUST 2:1071-1074, December 5, 1970.

"Immunoglobulins in spontaneous abortion and ectopic pregnancy," by R. T. O'Neill, et al. OBSTET GYNEC 36:264-267, August, 1970.

"The impact of the Abortion Act 1967 in Great Britain," by P. H.

Addison. MEDICOLEG J 38:15-21, 1970.

Importance of the fundamentals: practical key points in practice of therapeutic abortion," by M. Iwata. SANFUJIN JISSAI 19:339-345, April, 1970,

Importance of toxoplasmosis in abortion," by P. Spanio. MINERVA GINECOL 21:693-694, May 31, 1969.

Improving the quality of life," by C. E. Flowers Jr. ALA J MED SCI 7:297-299, July, 1970.

Incidence of malformations after threatened abortion," by A. Weidenbach, et al. ZENTRALBL GYNAEKOL 92:1594-1599, November 28, 1970.

Indication for Shirodkar's cervix cerclage," by S. Rageth. GEBURTSH FRAUENHEILK 30:236-239, March, 1970.

Induced abortion and its consequences," by S. Sasu. MUNCA SANIT 18:157-160, March, 1970.

Induced abortion in Lebanon," by W. M. Bickers. J MED LIBAN 23: 467-470, 1970.

Induced abortion in the Maternal-Child Institute," by L. E. Santamariã Páez. REV COLUMBIA OBSTET GINEC 21:137-139, March-April, 1970.

Induced abortion in a municipal hospital," by H. Schulman. OBSTET GYNECOL 36:616-620, October, 1970.

Induction of abortion by prostaglandins E1 and E2," by M. P. Embrey. BRIT MED J 1:258-260, May 2, 1970.

Induction of abortion using high doses of oxytocin," by J. Kopečný, et al. CESK GYNEK 35:118-119, March, 1970.

Induction of therapeutic abortion with intravenous prostaglandin F," by N. Wiqvist, et al. LANCET 1:889, April 25, 1970.

Infection of the fetus by Candida in a spontaneous abortion," by C. Y. Ho, et al. AMER J OBSTET GYNEC 106:705-710, March, 1970.

"Inflammation of genitalia following artificial pregnancy interruption," by J. Diviš, et al. CESK GYNEK 35:371-372, July, 1970.

"Influence of 1st pregnancy interruption on later gestation," by P. Heczko, et al. CESK GYNEK 35:333.334, July, 1970.

"The influence of medical and biological progress: the contemporary criminal law of abortion," by D Bein. in Feller, S. Z., ed. ISRAELI REPORTS TO THE EIGHTH INTERNATIONAL CONGRI OF COMPARATIVE LAW, 1970, 196-203.

"Influence of ornithine 8-vasopressin preparation upon blood loss afte induced abortions performed under local anesthesia," by J. Higier et al. GINEK POL 41:731-734, July, 1970.

"Inherited 13/14 chromosome translocation as a cause of human fetal wastage," by R. S. Sparkes, et al. OBSTET GYNEC 35:601;607, April, 1970.

"Insertion of IUD following artificial abortion," by J. Koukal, et al. CESK GYNEKOL 35:465-467, October, 1970.

"Insufficiency of the cervix uteri in relation to previous pregnancy in ruption," by V. Fuchs, et al. CESK GYNEK 35:365-367, July, 19

"Insufficiency of the uterine neck during pregnancy," by R. Wawryk. GEBURTSHILFE GYNAEKOL 173:212-217, 1970.

"Interruption graviditatis and lysis manualis placentae," by V. Bruta et al. CESK GYNEK 35:335-336, July, 1970.

"Interruption of late term pregnancy by means of vaginal cesarean se tion," by Z. Ia. Gendon. AKUSH GINEK 46:58-61, January, 1970

"Interruption of pregnancy before the period of fetal viability. The op ion of the national medical council about the abortion," PRESSE 78:2147-2149, November 14, 1970.

"Intrauterine curettage and the capacity of blood coagulation," by N. Shinagawa, et al. SANFUJIN JISSAI 19:758-762, July, 1970.

"Is abortion a right? symposium," CHR CENT 87:624-631, May 29, 1970; Discussion 87:972-973, August 12, 1970.

Is pregnancy interruption necessary following failure of the intrauterine device (IUD)," by M. Kohoutek, et al. CESK GYNEK 35:341-342, July, 1970.

Is therapeutic abortion preventable?" by W. Droegemueller, et al. OBSTET GYNEC 35:758-759, May, 1970.

Isolating the male bias against reform of abortion legislation," SANTA CLARA LAW 10:301, Spring, 1970.

Isthmic diseases and habitual abortion. Importance of isthmectomy," by F. Salvi. MINERVA GINECOL 21:679-681, May 31, 1969.

Isthmus encircling by abdominal route, apart from pregnancy, with an aponeurosis band in habitual abortions," by J. Y. Gillet, et al. BULL FED GYNEC OBSTET FRANC 22:132-134, January-March, 1970.

Isthmus insufficiency treated by cerclage operation," by K. Bang. UGESKR LAEG 132:734-736, April, 16, 1970.

It's alright, Ma (I'm only bleeding) (views on abortion), by Washington, D. C., Women's liberation. MOTIVE 30:33-38, March, 1970.

Japan wants to tighten its abortion law," MUCHEN MED WSCHR 29:2, July 17, 1970.

Jet-service abortion," by J. Dingman. CHATELAINE 43:4, June, 1970.

Kovacs' semiconservative method of pregnancy interruption," by I. Vido, et al. CESK GYNEK 35:345-347, July, 1970.

Late hemorrhage following undetected uterine ruptures during pregnancy interruptions," by J. Andrýs, et al. CESK GYNEK 35:364-365, July, 1970.

Law, preventive psychiatry, and therapeutic abortion," by H. I. Levene, et al. J NERV MENT DIS 151:51-59, July, 1970.

Legal abortion," by K. Soiva. DUODECIM 86:1295-1297, 1970.

Legal abortion. On handling it in antenatal institutions and hospitalization problems with commentary on development of new abortion laws," by M. Landgreen. UGESKR LAEG 132:347-353, February 12, 1970.

"Legal abortion and medical ethics," by L. Ribeiro. HOSPITAL 78: 439-476, August, 1970.

"Legal abortion and social class," by W. H. James. LANCET 2:658, September 26, 1970.

"Legal abortion without hospitalization," by A. J. Margolis, et al. OBSTET GYNEC 36:479-481, September, 1970.

"Legal abortions at the Stockholm General Maternity Hospital in 1967 1968," by J. Abolins, et al. LAKARTIDNINGEN 67:4039-4045, September 2, 1970.

"Legal abortions in Norway 1965-1969," by B. Grünfeld, et al. T NOF LAEGEFOREN 90:1261-1266, June 15, 1970.

"Legalized abortion: murder or mercy?" IMPRINT 17:12, January, 19

"Liberal abortion law, effective today, stirs worries in New York (N.Y doctors, hospitals fear they will be overwhelmed," by Peggy J. Murrell. WALL ST J 176:1+, July, 1, 1970.

"Listeriosis as cause of abortion," by R. Lange, et al. ZENTRALBL GYNAEKOL 92:313-318, March 7, 1970.

"Long-term follow up of secondary sterility following artificial interruption of pregnancy," by O. Kolářová. CESK GYNEKOL 35:399- September, 1970.

"Looking back at Luenbach: 296 non-hospital abortions. (Luenbach J by E. B. Keemer Jr. J NAT MED ASS 62:291-293, July, 1970.

"Macroscopic changes in the placenta after numerous induced abortions," by B. Kh. Aronov. AKUSH GINEKOL 46:72-73, July, 197

"Male use of contraception and attitudes toward abortion, Santiago, Chile, 1968 (responses in a survey)" by M.-Francoise Hall. MILBANK MEMORIAL FUND Q 48:145-166, April, 1970.

"The management of missed abortion," by G. J. Ratten. AUST NZ J OBSTET GYNAECOL 10:115-118, May, 1970.

"The massacre of the innocents: apropos of a proposed law to legaliz abortions under many circumstances," by E. Aubertin. BORDEAU MED 3:1873-1882, July-August, 1970.

26

"Maternal deaths due to sepsis with septic shock," OHIO MED J 66:589-591, June, 1970.

"Maternal mortality," J KENTUCKY MED ASS 68:416, July, 1970.

"Medical correlates of termination of use of intrauterine contraceptive devices in Taichung," by J. Y. Peng, et al. INT J FERTIL 15:120-126, April-June, 1970.

"Medical grand rounds at Yale-New Haven Hospital. Septic abortion," by F. L. Sachs, et al. CONN MED 34:649-653, September, 1970.

"Menstruation disorders following artificial interruption of pregnancy," by F. Mackŭ, et al. CESK GYNEKOL 35:401-402, September, 1970.

"Mental and sexual problems related to pregnancy interruption," by O. Kolářová. CESK GYNEK 35:378-379, July, 1970.

'Microbial findings in isthmus and cervix insufficiency and their significance for the therapeutic result of cerciage (preliminary report)," by I. Penev, et al. AKUSH GINEKOL (Sofiia) 9:94-100, 1970.

'Mr. Irvine's bill," LANCET 1:343-344, February 4, 1970.

'The moral muddle," CATH NURSE 32:4-5, June, 1970.

'Morality of abortion; views of D. Callahan," by K. L. Woodward. NEWSWEEK 75:64-65, June 8, 1970.

'Morphological study of human embryos with chromosome aberrations," by C. Roux. PRESSE MED 78:647-652, March 21, 1970.

'Most frequent complications of artificial pregnancy interruption within 10 years," by K. Zák. CESK GYNEK 35:367-368, July, 1970.

'My thoughts about abortion and premature births," by N. Tsutsumi. KANGO 22:184-186, March, 1970.

'Mycoplasma hominis and abortion," by H. J. Harwick, et al. J INFECT DIS 121:260-268, March, 1970.

'National guide to legal abortion," by L. Lader. LADIES HOME J 87:73, July, 1970.

"Natural law institute 1970: abortion. Recent statutes and the crime of abortion," by B. F. Brown; "Abortion: a human problem," by W. J. Kenealy; "Abortion: a moral or medical problem?" by L. Salzman. LOYOLA L REV 16:275, 1969-1970.

"A necessity in clinical supervision: hourly per abortum and per partum thermal curves," by G. Bruniquel. BULL FED GYNEC OBSTET FRANC 22:119-121, January-March, 1970.

"The new Abortion Act," T SYGEPL 70:218, May, 1970.

"The new abortion laws: How are they working?" TODAY'S HLTH 48: 21+, March, 1970.

"New biology and the prenatal child," by D. W. Brodie. J FAMILY L 9:391, 1970.

"New Mexico's 1969 criminal abortion law," by J. B. Sutin. NATURAL RESOURCES J 10:591, July, 1970.

"New problems and old ones back again," LANCET 2:872-873, October 24, 1970.

"Not fit to print? New York bishops' pastoral letter," by S. J. Adamo. AMERICA 123:568-570, December 26, 1970.

"Number one method," NATION 210:69-70, January 26, 1970.

"Observation of tissue antibodies in artificial pregnancy interruption," by A. Kotásek, et al. CESK GYNEK 35:356-357, July, 1970.

"Occurrence of ectopic pregnancy following artificial abortion," by F. Macků, et al. CESK GYNEK 35:375-377, July, 1970.

"Oestrogen and pregnanediol excretion in various obstetrical populations," by J. B. Brown, et al. PROC R SOC MED 63:1092-1095, November, 1970.

"1,229 cases of abortion in the Caldas University Hospital," by O. Vélez Ramirez. REV COLUMBIA OBSTET GINEC 21:147-179, March-April, 1970.

"Only her doctor knows," CHR TODAY 14:35-36, April 24, 1970.

"Open letter to American doctors," AMERICA 122:490-491, May 9, 19

"Oral administration of an association of an antibiotic enzymes and balsam in septic inflammatory diseases in gynecology and obstetrics," by G. Locardi. MINERVA MED 61:961-965, March 10, 1970.

The origin of human life," T ZIEKENVERPL 23:32-36, January 6, 1970.

Our experience with anesthesia in artificial pregnancy interruption," by K. Hrazdil. CESK GYNEK 35:349-350, July, 1970.

Our experience with the IUD (contraceptive loop) inserted immediately after interruption of pregnancy," by Z. Szereday, et al. ORV HETIL 111:2299-2300, September 27, 1970.

Out from under, women unite!" by K. Keate. SAT N 85:15-20, July, 1970.

Outcome of labor for the mother and child after pregnancy complicated by threatened abortion," by L. V. Ananich. VOPR OKHR MATERIN DET 15:68-71, November, 1970.

Panorama of abortion across the ages," by L. Fortier. UNION MED CAN 98:1534-1539, September, 1969.

Papal fallibility," CHR CENT 87:1309, November 4, 1970: Discussion 88:21, January 6, 1971.

Paracervical block anaestheis for the evacuation of incomplete abortion--a controlled trial," by W. R. Chatfield, et al. J OBSTET GYNAEC BRIT COMM 77:462-463, May, 1970.

Parental chromosomal aberrations associated with multiple abortions and an abnormal infant," by L. Y. Hsu, et al. OBSTET GYNECOL 36:723-730, November, 1970.

Pathogenesis, clinical aspects and therapy of inflammatory diseases of female genitalia, puerpera and postabortic septic diseases," AKUSH GINEK 46:21-31, April, 1970.

People v. Belous (Cal) 458 P 2d 194," FORDHAM L REV 38:557, March, 1970; HARV CIVIL RIGHTS L REV 5:133, January, 1970; ND L REV 46:249, Winter, 1970; TEMP L Q 43:302, Spring, 1970; U RICHMOND L REV 4:351, Spring, 1970; WASH U L Q 1969:445, Fall, 1969; WASHBURN L J 9:286, Winter, 1970.

Peritoneal puncture in emergency traumatology," SOINS 15:357-358 passim, September-October, 1970.

"Perverse observations on abortion," by P. J. Weber. CATH WORLD 212:74-77, November, 1970.

"Physician attitudes toward hospital abortion in Georgia--1970," by G Freeman, et al. J MED ASSOC GA 59:437-446, December, 1970.

"Physicians' attitudes on the abortion law. Report of survey, 1969," b R. G. Smith, et al. HAWAII MED J 29:209-211, January-February, 1970.

"The place for anti-D gamma globulin in abortion," by R. F. Edwards. AUST NZ J OBSTET GYNAECOL 10:96-98, May, 1970.

"Placenta and chromosome aberrations in spontaneous abortion," by E Philippe, et al. PRESSE MED 78:641-646, March 21, 1970.

"Placental acetylcholine in induction of premature labor," by R. C. Goodlin. AMER J OBSTET GYNEC 107:429-431, June 1, 1970.

"Plasma progesterone levels during bougie-induced abortion in mid-pregnancy," by Y. Manabe. J ENDOCR 46:127-128, January, 1970.

"Plasma progesterone levels during saline-induced abortion," by W. G Wiest, et al. J CLIN ENDOCR 30:774-777, June, 1970.

"Population crisis and extremism," by H. H. Suter. SCIENCE 168:777 May 15, 1970.

"The position of the Conseil de l'Ordre on some current problems," by J. Bréhant. PRESSE MED 78:1522-1523, July 11, 1970.

"Possible isoimmunization following legal interruption of pregnancy," A. Pontuch, et al. CESK GYNEK 35:357-358, July, 1970.

"Postabortal and postpartum tetanus," by B. K. Adadevoh, et al. J OBSTET GYNAECOL BR COMMONW 77:1019-1023, November, 19

"Post-abortum hemorrhage caused by intravascula coagulation. Cure b hysterectomy," by J. Testart, et al. ANN CHIR 24:229-234, February, 1970.

"Practical management of septic abortion," by J. C. Caillouette, et a HOSP MED 6:29+, January, 1970.

"Pregnancy and labor in patients with interventricular and interarteria septal defects," by A. L. Beĭlin. AKUSH GINEKOL 46:16-19, May, 1970.

"Pregnancy and labor in women with isthmic-cervical insufficiency," by S. A. Galitskaia, et al. PEDIATR AKUSH GINEKOL 4:43-45, July-August, 1970.

"Pregnancy interruption by means of vibrodilation and vacuum aspiration," by J. Német, et al. ZBL GYNAEK 92:120-127, January 24, 1970.

"Pregnancy outcome of women whose application for pregnancy interruption had been rejected," by M. Kohoutek, et al. CESK GYNEK 35:340-341, July, 1970.

"The pregnosticon all-in test in abnormal pregnancy," by F. J. Gibbs. J MED LAB TECHNOL 27:492-494, October, 1970.

"Preliminary assessment of the 1967 Abortion Act in practice," by P. Diggory, et al. LANCET 1:287-291, February 7, 1970.

"Premature termination of pregnancy following previous artificial interruption of pregnancy," by P. Dráč, et al. CESK GYNEK 35:332-333, July, 1970.

"Preparing for abortion procedures," HOSPITALS 44:69, August 16, 1970.

"The present status of abortion laws: A statement by the New York Academy of Medicine prepared by the Committee on Public Health," BULL NY ACAD MED 46:281-285, April, 1970.

"Presentation of a coefficient of measuring cervico-isthmic incompetence," by M. Dumont, et al. BULL FED SOC GYNECOL OBSTET LANG FR 22:470-472, September-October, 1970.

"The preservation of life," by N. K. Brown, et al. JAMA 211:76-82, January 5, 1970.

"Prevention of hypothalamic habitual abortion by periactin," by E. Sadovsky, et al. HAREFUAH 78:332-334, April 1, 1970.

"Preventive cesarean section in women with habitual abortion," by J. Kopečný, et al. CESK GYNEKOL 35:579-580, November, 1970.

31

"Primary indication of surgical pregnancy interruption," by M. Chalupa, et al. CESK GYNEK 35:344-345, July, 1970.

"The problem of unwanted pregnancies," by J. Sturma, et al. CESK GYNEK 35:35-37, February, 1970.

"Problems in enforcement of the abortion law," by T. Matsuura. J JAP MED ASSOC 64:1191-1194, November 15, 1970.

"Problems of miscarriage," by K. Niemineva. KATILOLEHTI 75:198-202, May, 1970.

"Progestogen therapy in early pregnancy and associated congenital defects," by S. Dillon. PRACTITIONER 205:80-84, July, 1970.

"Prognosis and treatment of post-abortum acute renal insufficiency," by M. Legrain, et al. PRESSE MED 78:1565-1570, August 29, 1970.

"The prognosis of threatened abortion," by J. H. Evans, et al. MED J 2:165-168, July 25, 1970.

"Prognostic value of urinary hormonal determinations during pregnancy," by P. Gellé, et al. REV FR GYNECOL OBSTET 64:215-233, May, 1969.

"Propos on abortion: apropos of a recent book," by J. E. Marcel. GYNEC PRAT 21:235-242, 1970.

"Prostaglandins and the induction of labour or abortion," LANCET 1:927-928, May 2, 1970.

"Prostaglandins and spontaneous abortion," by S. M. Karim, et al. J OBSTET GYNAEC BRIT COMM 77:837-839, September, 1970.

"Prostaglandins for induction of therapeutic abortion," by U. Roth-Brandel, et al. LANCET 1:190-191, January 24,1970.

"Prostaglandins in fertility control," by S. M. Karim. LANCET 1:1115, May 23, 1970.

"Psychiatric experience with a liberalized therapeutic abortion law," by L. Marder. AMER J PSYCHIAT 126:1230-1236, March, 1970.

"Psychiatric indications for the termination of pregnancy," MED J AUST 2:1212-1213, December 19, 1970.

"Psychiatric indications for therapeutic abortion," by C. W. Butler. SOUTHERN MED J 63:647-650, June, 1970.

"Psychiatric indications or psychiatric justification of therapeutic abortion?" by E. Pfeiffer. ARCH GEN PSYCHIATRY 23:402-407, November, 1970.

"Psychologic and emotional consequences of elective abortion. A review," by G. S. Walter. OBSTET GYNEC 36:482-491, September, 1970 (161 ref.).

"Psychological and emotional indications for therapeutic abortion," by N. M. Simon. SEMIN PSYCHIAT 2,3:283-301, 1970.

"Psychological aspects of abortion in Czechoslovkia," by Z. Dytrych. J PSYCHIAT NURS 8:30-33, May-June, 1970.

"Psychological aspects of habitual abortion," by M. Silverman, et al. PSYCHIATR COMMUN 13:35-43, 1970.

"Psychosocial aspects of therapeutic abortion," by L. Marder, et al. SOUTHERN MED J 63:657-661, June, 1970.

"Psychosocial studies in family planning behavior in Central and Eastern Europe. A preliminary report of a developing program," by H. P. David. J PSYCHIATR NURS 8:28-33, September-October, 1970.

"Quantitative changes in plasmaa fibrinogen in women prepared for pregnancy interruption by intravenous injection of EACA," by E. Howorka, et al. PRZEGL LEK 26:378-390, March 18, 1970.

"Reasons for abortion," BRIT MED J 3:362, August 15, 1970.

"Reasons for abortion," by D. G. Clyne. BR MED J 3:769-770, September 26, 1970.

"Recommended standards for abortion services. Adopted by the Executive Board of the APHA at the 98th Annual Meeting in Houston, Texas, October 29, 1970.

"Reforming the abortion laws: a doctor looks at the case," by D. Cavanagh. AMERICA 122:406-411, April 18, 1970; Discussion 122: 571, May 30, 1970.

"Registrar General's supplement on abortion," by P. Kestelman. LANCET 2:566-567, September 12, 1970.

"The relationship between progesterone, uterine volume, intrauterine pressure, and clinical progress in hypertonic saline--induced abortions," by A. I. Csapo, et al. AM J OBSTET GYNECOL 108:950-955, November 15, 1970.

"Religious aspects and theology in therapeutic abortion," by J. E. Herndon. SOUTHERN MED J 63:651-654, June, 1970.

"Repeated or habitual abortions," Q MED REV 21:1-30, July, 1970 (61 ref.).

"Results of gestanon therapy in women with threatened and habitual abortion," by Ts. Despodova. AKUSH GINEKOL (Sofiia) 9:208-213, 1970.

"Reviewing the Abortion Act," by P. Draper. BRIT MED J 3:344, August 8, 1970.

"Rh immunisation and abortion," LANCET 2:141, July 18, 1970.

"Rhesus sensitization following abortion," by H. Finger, et al. DEUTSCH MED WSCHR 95:1025-1028, May 1, 1970.

"RhoGam--current status," by K. P. Russell. CALIF MED 113:44-45, December, 1970.

"Right not to be born; refusal to grant therapeutic abortion in case of rubella baby," by M. K. Sanders. HARPER 240:92-99, April, 1970.

"Right of action for injury to, or death of a woman who consented to abortion," by D. Evans. J MED ASSOC STATE ALA 40:334 passim, November, 1970.

"Right to live," by J. R. Quinn. AMERICA 123:56-57, August 8, 1970.

"The right to live," by J. Stallworthy. J ROY COLL GEN PRACT 19: 187-190, April, 1970.

"Right to privacy: does it allow a woman the right to determine whether to bear children?" AM U L REV 20:136, August, 1970.

"The RN panel of 500 tells what nurses think about abortion," RN 33:40-43, June, 1970.

"The role of fetal death in the process of therapeutic abortion induced by intra-amniotic injection of hypertonic saline," by L. Kovács, et al. J OBSTET GYNAECOL BR COMMONW 77:1132-1136, December, 1970.

"The role of human conscience in therapeutic abortion," by P. R. Sullivan. AM J PSYCHIATRY 127:250, August, 1970.

"The role of mycoplasmas in human reproductive failure," by R. B. Kundsin, et al. ANN NY ACAD SCI 174:794-797, October 30, 1970.

"The role of RhoGAM in therapeutic and spontaneous abortion," by C. Sprague. HAWAII MED J 29:450-451, July-August, 1970.

"Rotilan anesthesia in induced abortion," by I. A. Vainberg, et al. AKUSH GINEKOL 46:73, July, 1970.

"RSH Congress. The Abortion Act 1967 discussed," NURS MIRROR 130:13-15, June 26, 1970.

"Rubella and abortion laws," by W. A. Burns. MED LEG BULL 208:1-7, August, 1970.

"A ruptured angular pregnancy," by J. Salasc. BULL FED SOC GYNECOL OBSTET LANG FR 22:292-294, June-August, 1970.

"Saline versus glucose as a hypertonic solution for abortion," by W. Droegemueller, et al. AM J OBSTET GYNECOL 108:606-609, October 15, 1970.

"A scheme in the management of threatened abortion," by V. Ruiz Velasco, et al. GINEC OBSTET MEX 28:209-218, August, 1970.

"Scientific organization of the work of medical personnel in surgery for the interruption of early pregnancy," by A. A. Bagrov, et al. AKUSH GINEKOL 46:69-70, November, 1970.

"Searching of truth on abortion," by E. Hervet. GYNEC OBSTET 69: 287-295, May-July, 1970.

"Septic abortion and septic shock," by B. A. Santamarina, et al. CLIN OBSTET GYNECOL 13:291-304, June, 1970.

"Septic abortion-current management," by J. C. Caillouette. CALIF MED 113:44, December, 1970.

"Septic abortion with endotoxic shock," by D. Cavanagh, et al. AUST NZ J OBSTET GYNAECOL 10:160-166, August, 1970.

"Septic incomplete abortion. A retrospective study of twenty years' experience," by D. R. Ostergard, et al. OBSTET GYNEC 35:709-713, May, 1970.

"Septic shock," by L. Heller, et al. ZBL GYNAEK 92:111-119, January 24, 1970.

"Septic threatened abortion. A retrospective study of twenty years' experience," by J. G. Bradley, et al. OBSTET GYNEC 35:714-717, May, 1970.

"Sequelae of artificial interruption of pregnancy in juveniles," by O. Mandausová, et al. CESK GYNEKOL 35:402-404, September, 1970.

"Sequellae of artificial pregnancy interruption," by J. Houdek, et al. CESK GYNEC 35:368-369, July, 1970.

"Sequellae of artificial pregnancy interruption," by V. Skála. CESK GYNEK 35:370-371, July, 1970.

"Sequellae of artificial pregnancy interruption," by A. Kotásek. CESK GYNEK 35:325-328, July, 1970.

"Sex disorders following artificial pregnancy interruption," by F. Kohoutek, et al. CESK GYNEK 35:380-381, July, 1970.

"Sex ratio in human embryos obtained from induced abortion: histological examination of the gonad in 1,452 cases," by S. Lee, et al. AM J OBSTET GYNECOL 108:1294-1297, December 15, 1970.

"The share of complications of artificial pregnancy interruption in hospital morbidity," by V. Laně, et al CESK GYNEK 35:374-375, July, 1970.

"Should abortion laws be liberalized? interviews," ed. by C. Remsberg, et al. GOOD H 170:92-93+, March, 1970.

"Should the United States legalize abortions? Yes," by B. Packwood; "No," by J. R. Rarick. AMERICAN LEGION MAGAZINE 88:22-23, June, 1970.

"Significance of abortion and pregnancy interruption for the passage of fetal erythrocytes and anti Rh (D) antibody formation," by Z. Křikal, et al. CESK GYNEK 35:359-360, July, 1970.

"Significance of sterility following artificial interruption of pregnancy," by M. Kohoutek, et al. CESK GYNEKOL 35:398-399, September, 197(

"Similarly I will not-cause abortion," by R. D. Knapp Jr. J LA STATE MED SOC 122:297-301, October, 1970.

"A simple midcervical cerciage operation for cervical incompetence during pregnancy," by M. K. Shaalan. AMER J OBSTET GYNEC 107:969-970, July 15, 1970.

"Social workers and abortion," by E. F. Ford. WOM R REVOLUTION J LIBERATION 1,2:18-19, Winter, 1970.

"Some effects of abnormal karyotype on intra-uterine growth and development," by D. I. Rushton. J PATHOL 101:Pxi, August, 1970.

"Some observations regarding unwanted pregnancies and therapeutic abortions," by C. P. Kimball. OBSTET GYNEC 35:293-296, February, 1970.

"Some psychiatric aspects of abortion," by S. Fleck. J NERV MENT DIS 151:42-50, July, 1970 (42 ref.).

"Spontaneous abortion and human pesticide residues DDT and DDE," by J. A. O'Leary, et al. AM J OBSTET GYNECOL 108:1291-1292, December 15, 1970.

"Spontaneous and induced abortion. Report of a WHO scientific group," WHO TECH REP SER 461:3-51, 1970.

"Staphylococcal septicemia. Comments on a case of staphyoloccal septicemia," by I. Zorlescu. MUNCA SANIT 18:682-685, November, 1970.

"State of the abortion question," by R. F. Drinan. COMMONWEAL 92: 108-109, April 17, 1970; Reply with rejoinder, E. MacNeil 92:283+, June 12, 1970.

"State of fetus in women with threatened abortion," by W. I. Grisczenko, et al. GINEK POL 41:19-21, January, 1970.

"Statement on implementation of the New York State abortion law by the Committee on Public Health of the New York Academy of Medicine," BULL NY ACAD MED 46:674-675, September, 1970.

"Sterility following artificial interruption of 1st pregnancy," by K. Jirátko, et al. CESK GYNEKOL 35:397-398, September, 1970.

"Study of cause of natural abortion: based on the data on natural abortion in 1967 socioeconomic population survey," by T. Suganuma, et al. JAP J PUBLIC HEALTH NURSE 26:49-51, October, 1970.

"Study on the cause of natural abortion--based on the 1967 socio-economic population survey," by T. Suganuma, et al. JAP J MIDWIF 24:50-56, October, 1970.

"Successful surgical management of uterine anomalies in habitual abortions," by A. Zwinger, et al. CESK GYNEK 35:275-277, 1970.

"The suction curette in termination of pregnancy," by D. Pfanner, et al. MED J AUST 2:733, October 17, 1970.

"Surgery of isthmico-cervical insufficiency during pregnancy using the modified Szendi method," by M. A. Niiazova. AKUSH GINEK 46:35-38, January, 1970.

"Surgical nursing: Abortions and sterilizations," REGAN REP NURS L 11:1, June, 1970.

"Surgical treatment of cervical incompetence during pregnancy," by D. Kaskarelis, et al. INT SURG 53:296-299, April, 1970.

"Surgical treatment of uterine cervix incompetence by means of circular suture concomitant with the suturing of the lateral edges of the external orifice of the cervix uteri," by R. Wawryk, et al. GINEKOL POL 41:985-988, September, 1970.

"Surveillance of women following rejection of their application for artificial pregnancy interruption," by M. Zdímalová, et al. CESK GYNEK 35:338-340, July, 1970.

"Survey of therapeutic abortion committees," by K. D. Smith, et al. CRIM L Q 12:279, July, 1970.

"Survey on eugenics with special reference to public awareness," by T. Matsuura, et al. J JAP MED ASS 63:1516-1520, June 15, 1970.

"The Swedish abortion law and its application," by R. Lindelius. LAKARTIDNINGEN 67:5509-5519, November 18, 1970.

"Talk with two abortionists: interview," ed. by B. Buresh. NEWSWEEK 75:61, April 13, 1970.

"Techniques of abortion," by W. J. Cameron. J KANS MED SOC 71: 375-377, October, 1970.

"Teratogenic effects of inhalation anesthetics," by V. Askrog, et al. NORD MED 83:498-500, April, 1970.

"Termination hysterectomy," by A. C. Lewis, et al. J OBSTET GYNAEC BRIT COMM 77:743-747, August, 1970.

"Termination of pregnancy," by D. M. Potts. BRIT MED BULL 26:65-71, January, 1970 (60 ref.).

"Termination of pregnancy on psychiatric grounds," by J. Johnson. MANCH MED GAZ 49:10, July, 1970.

"Therapeutic abortion," CALIF NURSE 66:1, December, 1970.

"Therapeutic abortion," by P.G. Coffey. CAN MED ASSOC J 103:1194 passim, November 21, 1970.

"Therapeutic abortion," by C.P. Harrison. CANAD MED ASS J 102: 1209-1211, May 30, 1970.

"Therapeutic abortion," by W. H. Pearse. NEBRASKA NURSE 3:6-7, May, 1970.

"Therapeutic abortion," by J. Stallworthy. PRACTITIONER 204:393-400, March, 1970.

"Therapeutic abortion. Clinical aspects," by E. C. Senay. ARCH GEN PSYCHIATRY 23:408-415, November, 1970.

"Therapeutic abortion. A two-year experience in one hospital," by H. Thompson, Et al. JAMA 213:991-995, August 10, 1970.

"Therapeutic abortion. Washington, D. C." by E. J. Connor, et al. MED ANN DC 39,3:133-137 & 186, 1970.

"Therapeutic abortion by local administration of prostaglandin," by N. Wiqvist, et al. LANCET 2:716-717, October 3, 1970.

"Therapeutic abortion in a Canadian city," by R. M. Boyce, et al. CAN MED ASSOC J 103:461-466, September 12, 1970.

"Therapeutic abortion in Great Britain," by D. A. Pond. SEMIN PSYCHIAT 2,3:336-340, 1970.

"Therapeutic abortion--the other side of the coin," by Z. M. Lebensohn. MED ANN DC 39:275-277, May, 1970.

"Therapeutic abortion using prostaglandin F2 alpha," by S. M. Karim, et al. LANCET 1:157-159, January 24, 1970.

"Therapeutic abortion--Washington, D. C." by E. J. Connor, et al. MED ANN DC 39:133-137 passim, March, 1970.

"Therapeutic abortion--who may have it?" by N. N. Chowdhury. J INDIAN MED ASS 54:163-164, February, 1970.

"Therapeutic abortions at University Hospitals, 1951-1969, with emphasis on current trends," by D. W. Wetrich, et al. J IOWA MED SOC 60:691-696, October, 1970.

"Therapeutic abortions, 1963-1968," by C. Tietze. STUDIES IN FAMIL PLANNING 59:5-7, November, 1970.

"Therapeutic abortions using prostaglandin E2," by G. M. Filshie. J REPROD FERTIL 23:371-372, November, 1970.

"Therapy of threatened abortion with progestational hormones," by G. Γ Montanari, et al. MINERVA GINECOL 21:683-684, May 31, 1969.

"Thiophenicol in current gynecological and obstetrical pathology," by M Cathely. REV FR GYNECOL OBSTET 64:293-295, May, 1969.

"The threat of Rh immunisation from abortion," by V. J. Freda, et al. LANCET 2:147-148, July 18, 1970.

"Threatened pregnancies," by Gregoire. BULL SOC SCI MED GRAND DUCHE LUXEMB 107:277-286, October, 1970.

"To be or not to be: the constitutional question of the California abortion law," U PA L REV 118:643, February, 1970

"To be or not to be: some thoughts on abortion," by M. Slatin. NEBRASKA NURSE 3:8-9, May, 1970.

"Toxoplasma antibodies in the blood of healthy and aborted women," by H. Ekmen. TURK HIJ TEER BIYOL DERG 30:56-62, 1970.

"Toxoplasmosis: abortions and stillbirths," by V. Hingorani, et al. INDIAN J MED RES 58:967-974, July, 1970.

"Toxoplasmosis and abortion. Serologic findings and clinical results," by M. Mega, et al. MINERVA GINECOL 21:694-695, May 31, 1969.

"Trans-abdominal cerclage in isthmic incontinence," by L. Ardillo.

MINERVA GINECOL 21:688-692, May 31, 1969.

'Transplacental haemorrhage after abortion," by J. M. Bowman. LANCET 1:1108, May 23, 1970.

'Transplacental haemorrhage after abortion," by S. Murray, et al. LANCET 1:631-634, March 28, 1970.

'Transplacental haemorrhage after abortion," by G. Neubauer. LANCET 1:952, May 2, 1970.

'Transplacental haemorrhage due to termination of pregnancy," by J. J. Walsh, et al. J OBSTET GYNAEC BRIT COMM 77:133-136, February, 1970.

'Transplacental hemorrhage during spontaneous and therapeutic artificial abortion," by J. A. Goldman, et al. OBSTET GYNEC 35:903-908, June, 1970.

'Transplacental hemorrhage in patients subjected to therapeutic abortion," by T. H. Parmley, et al. AMER J OBSTET GYNEC 106:540-542, February 15, 1970.

'Treatment of abortion with progesterone and etiology of abortion," by M. Sakurabayashi. J JAP OBSTET GYNEC SOC 22:69-72, January, 1970.

'Treatment of septic abortion and septic shock," by B. A. Santamarina, et al. MOD TREAT 7:779-788, July, 1970.

'Treatment of threatened abortion with high doses of progesterone," by P. Spanio, et al. MINERVA GINECOL 21:681-682, May 31, 1969.

'Treatment of too early delivery by alcohol," by P. Bergsjo. T NORSK LAEGEFOREN 90:36-37, January 1, 1970.

'Troubled waters," by M. T. Southgate. JAMA 213:1182-1183, August 17, 1970.

'The truth about abortion in New York," by R. E. Hall. COLUMBIA FORUM 13:18-22, Winter, 1970.

'Tubal ligation and abortion in the State of Alabama," by C. E. Flowers Jr. J MED ASS ALABAMA 39:945-947, April, 1970.

41

"Twin survival in therapeutic abortion," by C. P. Douglas. BR MED J 3:769, September 26, 1970.

"2 cases of post-abortion psychoses," by W. Pasini, et al. ANN MEDICOPSYCHOL 1:555-564, April, 1970.

"2 cases of post abortum perfringens septicemia. Death," by P. L. Barraya, et al. BULL FED SOC GYNECOL OBSTET LANG FR 22 354-355, June-August, 1970.

"Unusual case of intestinal lesions after induced abortion. Accidental finding in extragenital pathology," by F. Perretti. MINERVA GINE 22:252-255, February 28, 1970.

"Unusual sequel to therapeutic abortion," by R. McDonald. LANCET 1118, May 23, 1970.

"Up for approval," LANCET 1:760-761, April 11, 1970.

"Urinary chorionic gonadotropin excretion in pregnant women treated b cause of uterine cervix incompetency," by R. Wawryk, et al. GINE POL 41:851-855, 1970.

"Use of a combination of an antibiotic with proteolytic enzymes in pos abortion pelvic infection," by E. Acosta Bendek. GINEC OBSTET MEX 27:297-305, March, 1970.

"The use of hyperbaric oxygen in the treatment of clostridial septicem complicating septic abortion. Report of a case," by L. E. Perrin, e al. AMER J OBSTET GYNEC 106:666-668, March, 1970.

"Use of mechanohysterography in the diagnosis of threatened miscarri in women's consultation centers," by I. M. Griaznova, et al. VOP OKHR MATERIN DETS 15:64-67, February, 1970.

"Use of prostaglandin E2 for therapeutic abortion," by S. M. Karim, et BRIT MED J 1:198-200, July 25, 1970.

"Uses of amniocentesis," by J. H. Edwards. LANCET 1:608-609, March 21, 1970.

"Use of prostaglandin E2 in the management of missed abortion, misse labour, and hydatidiform mole," by S. M. Karim. BRIT MED J 1:19 197, July 25, 1970.

"The use of suction curettage in incomplete abortion," by P. E. Suter et al. J OBSTET GYNAEC BRIT COMM 77:464-466, May, 1970.

"The uterine cervix following artificial pregnancy interruption," by K. Sapâk, et al. CESK GYNEK 35:355-356, July, 1970.

"Uterus injury in artificial pregnancy interruption and its sequellae," by V. Nesit. CESK GYNEK 35:360-362, July, 1970.

"Uterus perforation as a complication of legal pregnancy interruption," by R. Kronus, et al. CESK GYNEK 35:362-364, July, 1970.

"Vacuum aspiration for the therapeutic abortion," by H. Jenssen. T NORSK LAEGEFOREN 90:19-21, January 1, 1970.

"Vacuum aspiration in therapeutic abortion," by B. Barmen. T NORSK LAEGEFOREN 90:15-16, January 1, 1970.

"Vacuum aspiration in therapeutic and incomplete abortion," by J. C. Aure. T NORSK LAEGEFOREN 90:16-18, January 1, 1970.

"Vacuum aspiration of the uterus in therapeutic abortion," by A. E. Buckle, et al. BRIT MED J 1:456-457, May 23, 1970.

"Vacuum curettage. Out patient curettage without anasthesia. A report of 350 cases," by J. G. Jensen. DAN MED BULL 17,7:199-209, 1970.

"The value of human abortuses in the surveillance of developmental anomalies. I. General overview," by J. R. Miller, et al. CAN MED ASSOC J 103:501-502, September 12, 1970.
"II, Reduction deformities of the limbs," by J. R. Miller, et al. CAN MED ASSOS J 103:503-505, September 12, 1970.

"Various problems involving the abortion law. Evaluation of the results of the study of its practice," by T. Yoshikawa. JAP J MIDWIFE 24: 31-34, December, 1970.

"Veto for abortion; Maryland," NEWSWEEK 75:51-52, June 8, 1970.

"Victims: interviews," RAMP MAG 9:23-25, August, 1970.

"Visual function in septic abortion," by E. I. Khvat. VESTN OFTALMOL 5:89-90, 1970.

"Voluntary abortion," by R. Mahon BULL INFIRM CATHOL CAN

37:219-225, September-December, 1970.

"War on the womb," CHR TODAY 14:24-25, June 5, 1970.

"Washington abortion reform," by GONZAGA L REV 5:270, Spring, 197

"What men should be told about abortion," by N. V. Don. FELDSH AKU
35:45-46, June, 1970.

"What's wrong with abortion?" by F. W. Zanden, et al. J W AUST NUR
36:22 passim, June, 1970.

"When abortion is made easier: more and more states are discovering
what happens when abortion laws are relaxed; demand is rising to
make such operations, by licensed physicians, more available; even
a national law is proposed," U S NEWS 68:83, June 8, 1970.

"Whither therapeutic abortion?" by D. Hay. MANCH MED GAZ 50:7-10
passim, October, 1970.

"Whole world off her back; the Dorene Falk case," NEWSWEEK 75:54-
April 13, 1970.

"Why women are *still* angry over abortion," by M. Gillen. CHATELAIN
43:34-35,80+, October, 1970.

"Will she, won't she?" by H. W. Ashworth. MANCHESTER MED GAZ
49:7, March, 1970.

"Women are turning on the heat," by G. Pape. MON TIMES 138:46,
June, 1970.

"The W.M.A. statement on therapeutic abortion," MED J AUST 2:484-
485, September 12, 1970.

"Work of the commission for pregnancy interruption in Berlin," by L.
Waldeyer. DEUTSCH GESUNDH 25:28-32, January 9, 1970.

"You may be right. Therapeutic abortion in medical perspective," by
J. E. Hodgson. MINN MED 53:755 passim, July, 1970.

SUBJECT INDEX

ADOPTION
   see: Family Planning

ABNORMALITIES
   see: Complications

ABORTION ACT
   see: Laws and Legislation

ANESTHESIA
   see also: Induced Abortion
            Therapeutic Abortion

"Analysis of blood loss in artificial termination of pregnancy under
   local anesthesia," by J. Higier, et al. WIAD LEK 23:1289-1293,
   August 1, 1970.

"The effects of anesthesia and pulmonary ventilation on blood loss
   during elective therapeutic abortion," by B. F. Cullen, et al.
   ANESTHESIOLOGY 32:108-113, February, 1970.

"Effects of anesthesia in therapeutic abortion," by W. H. Forrest, Jr.
   ANESTHESIOLOGY 33:121-122, July, 1970.

"Experience in anesthesia for artificial interrupting of pregnancy by a
   new intravenous anesthetic, propanidid (Epontol)," by K. Nagauchi,
   et al. SANFUJIN JISSAI 19:873-876, August, 1970.

"Influence of ornithine 8-vasopressin preparation upon blood loss
   after induced abortions performed under local anesthesia," by
   J. Higier, et al. GINEK POL 41:731-734, July, 1970.

"Our experience with anesthesia in artificial pregnancy interruption,"

ANESTHESIA

by K. Hrazdil. CESK GYNEK 35:349-350, July, 1970.

"Paracervical block anaesthesia for the evacuation of incomplete abortion--a controlled trial," by W. R. Chatfield, et al. J OBSTET GYNAEC BRIT COMM 77:462-463, May, 1970.

"Rotilan anesthesia in induced abortion," by I. A. Vainberg, et al. AKUSH GINEKOL 46:73, July, 1970.

"Teratogenic effects of inhalation anesthesia," by V. Askrog, et al. NORD MED 83:498-500, April 16, 1970.

ANTIBODIES
"Artificial abortion and immunization with antigens A or B in women with blood group O," by M. Jakubowska, et al. POL TYG LEK 25:1263-1264, August 17, 1970.

"Observation of tissue antibodies in artificial pregnancy interruption, by A. Kotásek, et al. CESK GYNEK 35:356-357, July, 1970.

"Toxoplasma antibodies in the blood of healthy and aborted women," by H. Ekmen. TURK HIJ TECR BIYOL DERG 30:56-62, 1970.

ARTIFICIAL INTERRUPTION
see: Induced Abortion

BEHAVIOR
see: Sociology

CANDIDIASIS
"Infection of the fetus by Candida in a spontaneous abortion," by C. Y. Ho, et al. AMER J OBSTET GYNEC 106:705-710, March, 1970.

CEPHALORIDINE
"Cephaloridine in septic abortion. Comparison with a conventional combined antibiotic regimen in a conservative program of management," by W. E. Josey, et al. AMER J OBSTET GYNEC 106: 237-242, January 15, 1970.

CERVICAL INCOMPETENCE OR INSUFFICIENCY

"An abortion with an unusual course (cervical pregnancy)," by J. Richon, et al. BULL FED SOC GYNECOL OBSTET LANG FR 22:243-246, April-May, 1970.

"Cervical incompetence in multiple pregnancy," by G. W. McGowan. OBSTET GYNEC 35:589-591, April, 1970.

"Cervical insufficiency," by O. Hirokawa. SAISHIN IGAKU 25:671-674, March, 1970.

"Cervical insufficiency in pregnancy. McDonald's surgical method," by P. Rössner. DTSCH GESUNDHEITSW 25:750-754, April 23, 1970.

"Definitive treatment for incompetent cervix," by G. P. Charlewood. S AFR MED J 44:1367-1368, November 28, 1970.

"The dermal graft and cervical incompetency," by J. L. Breen. INT J FERTIL 15:1-13, January-March, 1970.

"Evaluation of results of surgical treatment of cervical isthmus insufficiency being the cause of late abortions and miscarriages," by W. Kokoszka, et al. PRZEGL LEK 26:769-770, 1970.

"Failures of cervix uteri cerclage due to a fault of technic," by M. Dumont, et al. BULL FED SOC GYNECOL OBSTET LANG FR 22:473, September-October, 1970.

"Habitual abortion and premature labor caused by primary cervical insufficiency. Surgical and pharmacological treatment," by G. Colucci, et al. MINERVA GINECOL 21:687-688, May 31, 1969.

"Indication for Shirodkar's cervix cerclage," by S. Rageth. GEBURTSH FRAUENHEILK 30:236-239, March, 1970.

"Insufficiency of the cervix uteri in relation to previous pregnancy interruption," by V. Fuchs, et al. CESK GYNEK 35:365-366, July, 1970.

"Insufficiency of the uterine neck during pregnancy," by R. Wawryk.

CERVICAL INCOMPETENCE OR INSUFFICIENCY

Z GEBURTSHILFE GYNAEKOL 173:212-217, 1970.

"Isthmus insufficiency treated by cerclage operation," by K. Bang. UGESKR LAEG 132:734-736, April 16, 1970.

"Microbial findings in isthmus and cervix insufficiency and their significance for the therapeutic result of cerclage (preliminary report)," by I. Penev, et al. AKUSH GINEKOL (Sofiia) 9:94-100 1970.

"Pregnancy and labor in women with isthmic-cervical insufficiency," by S. A. Galitskaia, et al. PEDIATR AKUSH GINEKOL 4:43-45, July-August, 1970.

"Presentation of a coefficient of measuring cervico-isthmic incompetence," by M. Dumont, et al. BULL FED SOC GYNECOL OBSTI LANG FR 22:470-472, September-October, 1970.

"A simple midcervical cerclage operation for cervical incompetence during pregnancy," by M. K. Shaalan. AMER J OBSTET GYNEC 107:969-970, July 15, 1970.

"Surgery of isthmico-cervical insufficiency during pregnancy using the modified Szendi method," by M. A. Niiazova. AKUSH GINEK 46:35-38, January, 1970.

"Surgical treatment of cervical incompetence during pregnancy," by D. Kaskarelis, et al. INT SURG 53:296-299, April, 1970.

"Surgical treatment of uterine cervix incompetence by means of circular suture concomitant with the suturing of the lateral edges of the external orifice of the cervix uteri," by R. Wawryk, et al. GINEKOL POL 41:985-988, September, 1970.

"Urinary chorionic gonadotropin excretion in pregnant women treated because of uterine cervix incompetency," by R. Wawryk, et al. GINEK POL 41:851-855, 1970.

"The uterine cervix following artificial pregnancy interruption, by K. Sapák, et al. CESK GYNEK 35:355-356, July, 1970.

CESAREAN SECTION
"Complication of hysterotomy," by S. V. Sood. BR MED J 4:495-496, November 21, 1970.

"Interruption of late term pregnancy by means of vaginal cesarean section," by Z. Ia. Gendon. AKUSH GINEK 46:58-61, January, 1970.

"Preventive cesarean section in women with habitual abortion," by J. Kopečný, et al. CESK GYNEKOL 35:579-580, November, 1970.

CLINICAL ASPECTS
"Abortion in the first trimester. Anatomico-clinical studies of 100 cases," by Esquivel A. Cerón, et al. GINECOL OBSTET MEX 28:449-461, October, 1970.

"Clinical and x-ray aspects of pulmonary edema in patients with sepsis following abortion," by Kh. A. Khidirbeil, et al. VESTN RENTGEN RADIOL 45:77-82, March-April, 1970.

"Clinical aspects of hormonal protection during pregnancy," by G. A. Hauser. NED TIJDSCHR VERLOSKD GYNAECOL 70:436-445, October, 1970.

"Clinical use of depressing agents," by J. S. Skjaeraasen. TIDSSKR NOR LAEGEFOREN 90:2192-2196, December 1, 1970.

"Clinical use of prostaglandins," BR MED J 4:253-254, October, 1970.

"Evaluation of the effectiveness of metacin therapy in threatened premature labor and late abortion (clinico-hysterographic study)," by M. Ia. Martynshin. AKUSH GINEK 46:39-43, January, 1970.

"A necessity in clinical supervision: hourly per abortum and per partum thermal curves," by G. Bruniquel. BULL FED GYNEC OBSTET FRANC 22:119-121, January-March, 1970.

"Pathogenesis, clinical aspects and therapy of inflammatory diseases of female genitalia, puerpera and postabortic septic diseases," AKUSH GINEK 46:21-31, April, 1970.

CLINICAL ASPECTS

"The relationship between progesterone, uterine volume, intra-uterine pressure, and clinical progress in hypertonic saline--induced abortions," by A. I. Csapo, et al. AM J OBSTET GYNECOL 108:950-955, November 15, 1970.

"Therapeutic abortion. Clinical aspects," by E. C. Senay. ARCH GE PSYCHIATRY 23:408-415, November, 1970.

"Toxoplasmosis and abortion. Serologic findings and clinical results," by M. Mega, et al. MINERVA GINECOL 21:694-695, May 31, 1969.

COMPLICATIONS

see also: Hemorrhage

"Abnormalities of early human development," by B. F. Stratford. AMER J OBSTET GYNEC 107:1223-1232, August 15, 1970.

"Abortion caused by chromosomal abnormalities and estrogen insufficiency of the corpus luteum," by J. Cohen. PRESSE MED 78:174 September 26, 1970.

"Anatomic and chromosomal anomalies in spontaneous abortion. Possible correlation with overripeness of oocytes," by K. Mikamo. AMER J OBSTET GYNEC 106:243-254, January 15, 1970.

"Association of maternal genital herpetic infection with spontaneous abortion," by Z. M. Naib, et al. OBSTET GYNEC 35:260-263, February, 1970.

"Atonic hemorrhage in pregnancy interruption and its complications due to coagulation disorders," by O. Vago. ZBL GYNAEK 92:62 63, January 10, 1970.

"Chromosome aberrations in spontaneous abortion," by P. Dráč, et al CESK GYNEK 35:230-233, May, 1970 (42 ref.).

"Complications in the interruption of abortion depending on the meth used--classical or aspiration method," by A. Atanasov. AKUSH GINEKOL (Sofiia) 9:271-277, 1970.

50

COMPLICATIONS

"The consequences of criminal abortion on the woman's state of
health," by M. Handru. MUNCA SANIT 18:345-348, June, 1970.

"Endometrium and the sequelae of abortion," by E. Philippe, et al.
REV FRANC GYNEC OBSTET 65:413-421, July-August, 1970.

"Evaluation of sequellae and possibilities of pregnancy interruption
by women who experienced it," by E. Dlhoš, et al. CESK GYNEK
35:336-338, July, 1970.

"Foreign body in the abdominal cavity," by A. Murdzhiev, et al.
AKUSH GINEKOL (Sofiia) 9:347-348, 1970.

"Foreign body in urinary bladder from attempted abortion," by G. S.
Bernstein, et al. OBSTET GYNEC 36:475-478, September, 1970.

"The formation of bone in uterine tissues," by A. Springer, et al. REV
FRANC GYNEC OBSTET 65:519-522, September, 1970.

"Hazards of 1st pregnancy interruptions," by L. Sokolik, et al.
CESK GYNEK 35:373-374, July, 1970.

"Hysterographic changes following uterine injury during artificial
interruption of pregnancy," by V. Nesit. CESK GYNEK 35:353-
354, July, 1970.

"Immunoglobulins in spontaneous abortion and ectopic pregnancy,"
by R. T. O'Neill, et al. OBSTET GYNEC 36:264-267, August,
1970.

"Incidence of malformations after threatened abortion," by A.
Weidenbach, et al. ZENTRALBL GYNAEKOL 92:1594-1599,
November 28, 1970.

"Inflammation of genitalia following artificial pregnancy interruption," by J. Diviš, et al. CESK GYNEK 35:371-372, July, 1970.

"Long-term follow up of secondary sterility following artificial interruption of pregnancy," by O. Kolářová. CESK GYNEKOL 35:399-
400, September, 1970.

"Menstruation disorders following artificial interruption of pregnancy," by F. Mackú, et al. CESK GYNEKOL 35:401-402, September, 1970

"Morphological study of human embryos with chromosome aberrations," by C. Roux. PRESSE MED 78:647-652, March 21, 1970.

"Most frequent complications of artificial pregnancy interruption withi 10 years," by K. Zák. CESK GYNEK 35:367-368, July, 1970.

"Mycoplasma hominis and abortion," by H. J. Harwick, et al. J INFECT DIS 121:260-268, March, 1970.

"Occurrence of ectopic pregnancy following artificial abortion," by F. Mackú, et al. CESK GYNEK 35:375-377, July, 1970.

"Parental chromosomal aberrations associated with multiple abortions and an abnormal infant," by L. Y. Hsu, et al. OBSTET GYNECOL 36:723-730, November, 1970.

"Placenta and chromosome aberrations in spontaneous abortion," by E. Philippe, et al. PRESSE MED 78:641-646, March 21, 1970.

"Postabortal and postpartum tetanus," by B. K. Adadevoh, et al. J OBSTET GYNAECOL BR COMMONW 77:1019-1023, November, 1970.

"A ruptered angular pregnancy," by J. Salasc. BULL FED SOC GYNECOL OBSTET LANG FR 22:292-294, June-August, 1970.

"Sequelae of artificial interruption of pregnancy in juveniles," by O. Mandausová, et al. CESK GYNEKOL 35:402-404, September, 1970.

"Sequellae of artificial pregnancy interruption," by J. Houdek, et al. CESK GYNEK 35:368-369, July, 1970.

"Sequellae of artificial pregnancy interruption," by A. Kotásek. CESK GYNEK 35:325-328, July, 1970.

"Sequellae of artificial pregnancy interruption," by V. Skála. CESK GYNEK 35:370-371, July, 1970.

COMPLICATIONS

"Sex disorders following artificial pregnancy interruption," by F. Kohoutek, et al. CESK GYNEK 35:380-381, July, 1970.

"The share of complications of artificial pregnancy interruption in hospital morbidity," by V. Laně, et al. CESK GYNEK 35:374-375, July, 1970.

"Sterility following artificial interruption of 1st pregnancy," by K. Jirátko, et al. CESK GYNEKOL 35:397-398, September, 1970.

"Successful surgical management of uterine anomalies in habitual abortions," by A. Zwinger, et al. CESK GYNEK 35:275-277, 1970.

"Trans-abdominal cerclage in isthmic incontinence," by L. Ardillo. MINERVA GINECOL ' 21:688-692, May 31, 1969.

"Unusual case of intestinal lesions after induced abortion. Accidental finding in extragenital pathology," by F. Perretti. MINERVA GINEC 22:252-255, February 28, 1970.

"Uterus injury in artificial pregnancy interruption and its sequellae," by V. Nesit. CESK GYNEK 35:360-362, July, 1970.

"Uterus perforation as a complication of legal pregnancy interruption," by R. Kronus, et al. CESK GYNEK 35:362-364, July, 1970.

"The value of human abortuses in the surveillance of developmental anomalies. I. General overview," by J. R. Miller, et al. CAN MED ASSOC J 103:501-502, September 12, 1970.
"II. Reduction deformities of the limbs," by J. R. Miller, et al. CAN MED ASSOC J 103:503-505, September 12, 1970.

CONTRACEPTION

"Chromosome studies in selected spontaneous abortion. 1. Conception after oral contraceptives," by D. H. Carr. CANAD MED ASS J 103:343-348, August 15, 1970.

"Contraception and abortion: American Catholic responses," by D. Callahan. AMERICAN ACADEMY OF POLITICAL AND SOCIAL SCIENCE 387:109-117, February, 1970.

CONTRACEPTION

"Fertility control: health and educational factors for the 1970s. Contraception or abortion?" by J. H. Hughes. J BIOSOC SCI 2:161-166, April, 1970.

"Insertion of IUD following artificial abortion," by J. Koukal, et al. CESK GYNEKOL 35:465-467, October, 1970.

"Is pregnancy interruption necessary following failure of the intrauterine device (IUD)," by M. Kohoutek, et al. CESK GYNEK 35: 341-342, July, 1970.

"Male use of contraception and attitudes toward abortion, Santiago, Chile, 1968 (responses in a survey)," by M. Francoise Hall. MILBANK MEMORIAL FUND Q 48:145-166, April, 1970.

"Medical correlates of termination of use of intrauterine contraceptiv devices in Taichung," by J. Y. Peng, et al. INT J FERTIL 15: 120-126, April-June, 1970.

"Our experience with the IUD (contraceptive loop) inserted immediate after interruption of pregnancy," by Z. Szereday, et al. ORV HETIL 111:2299-2300, September 27, 1970.

DIAGNOSIS
"Abortion reform: history, status, and prognosis," by W. Case. RES REV 21:521, April, 1970.

"Data of value in the prognosis of threatened abortion," by V. Ruiz Velasco, et al. REV OBSTET GINECOL VENEZ 30:109-124, 19

"Diagnostic error while using ultrasonic diagnosis in the question: extrauterine pregnancy or abortus imminens," by W. Nusch. GEBURTSHILFE FRAUENHEILKD 30:1120-1122, December, 19

"Effect of gestational and maternal age in early abortion," by D. T. Arakaki, et al. OBSTET GYNEC 35:264-269, February, 1970.

"Further course of gestation in women treated because of threatened abortion. Evaluation through vaginal smears," by R. Wawryk, et a GINEK POL 41:395-400, April, 1970.

54

"The pregnosticon all-in test in abnormal pregnancy," by F. J. Gibbs. J MED LAB TECHNOL 27:492-494, October, 1970.

"Prognosis and treatment of post-abortum acute renal insufficiency," by M. Legrain, et al. PRESSE MED 78:1565-1570, August 29, 1970.

"The prognosis of threatened abortion," by J. H. Evans, et al. MED J AUST 2:165-168, July 25, 1970.

"Prognostic value of urinary hormonal determinations during pregnancy," by P. Gellé, et al. REV FR GYNECOL OBSTET 64:215-233, May, 1969.

"Use of mechanohysterography in the diagnosis of threatened miscarriage in women's consultation centers," by I. M. Griaznova, et al. VOP OKHR MATERIN DETS 15:64-67, February, 1970.

DRUG THERAPY
see also: Techniques of Abortion

"Abortion and catecholamines," by T. K. Eskes. NED TIJDSCHR VERLOSKD GYNAECOL 70:465-474, October, 1970.

"Abortion caused by type II Herpesvirus. Isolation of the virus from cultures of zygotic tissues," by A. Boué, et al. PRESSE MED 78: 103-106, January 17, 1970.

"Abortion due to Pseudomonas aeruginosa. Protection of the pregnant guinea pig by vaccination," by R. Durieux, et al. GYNECOL OBSTET 69:301-308, August-October, 1970.

"Administration of epsilon-aminocaproic acid (EACA) in the prevention of fibrinolytic hemorrhages associated with the expulsion of the fetus remaining in the uterus after its death," by E. Howorka, et al. WIAD LEK 23:973-977, June, 1970.

"Apropos of embryotoxic and teratogenic actions of "triton W.R. 1339" in the mouse: influence of vitamin A," by C. Roussel, et al. C R ACAD SCI (D) 271:215-218, July 15, 1970.

"Attempt at abortion with potassium permanganate tablets," by A. Le Coz, et al. BULL FED SOC GYNECOL OBSTET LANG FR 20:190-191, April-May, 1968.

"Benzidamine and tetracycline therapy in gynecologic and obstetrical pathology," by L. Tinelli, et al. MINERVA GINECOL 22:677-680 July 15, 1970.

"Cephaloridine in septic abortion. Comparison with a conventional combined antibiotic regimen in a conservative program of management," by W. E. Josey, et al. AMER J OBSTET GYNEC 106:237-242, January 15, 1970.

"Clinical use of depressing agents," by J. S. Skjaeraasen. TIDSSKR NOR LAEGEFOREN 90:2192-2196, December 1, 1970.

"Comparison of two antibiotic regimens in the treatment of septic abortion," by D. R. Ostergard. OBSTET GYNEC 36:473-474, September, 1970.

"Contractibility of the human uterus and the hormonal situation. Studies on therapy with progesterone in pregnancy," by P. Mentasti, et al. MINERVA GINECOL 21:685-687, May 31, 1969.

"The effect of oxytocin on the complication rate of early therapeutic abortions," by E. D. B. Johansson. ACTA OBSTET GYNEC SCAND 49,2:129-131, 1970.

"Evaluation of the effectiveness of metacin therapy in threatened premature labor and late abortion (clinico-hysterographic study)," by M. Ia. Martynshin. AKUSH GINEK 46:39-43, January, 1970.

"Failure of large doses of ethinyl estradiol to interfere with early embryonic development in the human species," by M. Bačič, et al AMER J OBSTET GYNEC 107:531-534, June 15, 1970.

"High doses of progesterone in the therapy of hormonal abortion and the prevention of various types of pregnancy interruption," by C. Morra, et al. MINERVA GINECOL 21:699-701, May 31, 1969.

"Hypertonic saline induction of abortion," by R. C. Goodlin. JAMA 211:1544, March 2, 1970.

"Induction of abortion using high doses of oxytocin," by J. Kopečný, et al. CESK GYNEK 35:118-119, March, 1970.

"Oral administration of an association of an antibiotic, enzymes and balsam in septic inflammatory diseases in gynecology and obstetrics," by G. Locardi. MINERVA MED 61:961-965, March 10, 1970.

"The place for anti-D gamma globulin in abortion," by R. F. Edwards. AUST NZ J OBSTET GYNAECOL 10:96-98, May, 1970.

"Practical management of septic abortion," by J. C. Caillouette, et al. HOSP MED 6:29+, January, 1970.

"Prevention of hypothalamic habitual abortion by periactin," by E. Sadovsky, et al. HAREFUAH 78:332-334, April 1, 1970.

"Progestogen therapy in early pregnancy and associated congenital defects," by S. Dillon. PRACTITIONER 205:80-84, July, 1970.

"Quantitative changes in plasma fibrinogen in women prepared for pregnancy interruption by intravenous injection of EACA," by E. Howorka, et al. PRZEGL LEK 26:378-390, March 18, 1970.

"Results of gestanon therapy in women with threatened and habitual abortion," by Ts. Despodova. AKUSH GINEKOL (Sofiia) 9:208-213, 1970.

"RhoGam--current status," by K. P. Russell. CALIF MED 113:44-45, December, 1970.

"The role of fetal death in the process of therapeutic abortion induced by intra-amniotic injection of hypertonic saline," by L. Kovacs, et al. J OBSTET GYNAECOL BR COMMONW 77:1132-1136, December, 1970.

"Saline versus glucose as a hypertonic solution for abortion," by W. Droegemueller, et al. AM J OBSTET GYNECOL 108:606-609, October 15, 1970.

"Septic abortion--current management," by J. C. Caillouette. CALIF MED 113:44, December, 1970

"Therapy of threatened abortion with progestational hormones," by G. D. Montanari, et al. MINERVA GINECOL 21:683-684, May 31, 1969.

"Treatment of abortion with progesterone and etiology of abortion," M. Sakurabayashi. J JAP OBSTET GYNEC SOC 22:69-72, January, 1970.

"Treatment of threatened abortion with high doses of progesterone," by P. Spanio, et al. MINERVA GINECOL 21:681-682, May 31, 19

"Treatment of too early delivery by alcohol," by P. Bergsjo. T NOR LAEGEFOREN 90:36-37, January 1, 1970.

"Treatment of septic abortion and septic shock," by B. A. Santamar et al. MOD TREAT 7:779-788, July, 1970.

"Use of a combination of an antibiotic with proteolytic enzymes in post-abortion pelvic infection," by E. Acosta Bendek. GINEC OBSTET MEX 27:297-305, March, 1970.

"Uses of amniocentesis," by J. H. Edwards. LANCET 1:608-609, March 21, 1970.

EACA
"Administration of epsilon-aminocaproic acid (EACA) in the prevention of fibrinolytic hemorrhages associated with the expulsion of the fetus remaining in the uterus after its death," by E. Howorka et al. WIAD LEK 23:973-977, June, 1970.

"Quantitative changes in plasma fibrinogen in women prepared for pregnancy interruption by intravenous injection of EACA," by E Howorka, et al. PRZEGL LEK 26:378-390, March 18, 1970.

ETHINYL ESTRADIOL
"Failure of large doses of ethinyl estradiol to interfere with early embryonic development in the human species," by M. Bačič, et a AMER J OBSTET GYNEC 107:531-534, June 15, 1970.

FAMILY PLANNING
see also: Sociology

"Abortion and adoption," by C. Schoenberg. CHILD WELFARE 49: 544, December, 1970.

"Abortion and the unwanted child (United States): an interview with Alan F. Guttmacher, M.D., and Harriet F. Pilpel," FAMILY PLANNING PERSPECTIVES 2:16-24, March, 1970.

"Family planning counseling," by E. F. Daily. BRIT MED J 3:345-346, August 8, 1970.

"Freedom in family planning. The abortion law and women's liberation," by H. Muramatsu. JAP J MIDWIFE 24:10-19, December, 1970.

"Health insurance for abortion costs: a survey," by C. F. Muller. FAMILY PLANNING PERSPECTIVES 2:12-20, October, 1970.

"The problem of unwanted pregnancies," by J. Sturma, et al. CESK GYNEK 35:35-37, February, 1970.

"Psychosocial studies in family planning behavior in Central and Eastern Europe. A preliminary report of a developing program," by H. P. David. J PSYCHIATR NURS 8:28-33, September-October, 1970.

"Social workers and abortion," by E. F. Ford. WOM R REVOLUTION J LIBERATION 1,2:18-19, Winter, 1970.

"Some observations regarding unwanted pregnancies and therapeutic abortions," by C. P. Kimball. OBSTET GYNEC 35:293-296, February, 1970.

"Therapeutic abortions, 1963-1968," by C. Tietze. STUDIES IN FAMILY PLANNING 59:5-7, November, 1970.

FERTILITY
see: Sterility

FERTILIZATION
see also: Sterility or Sterilization

"Aging of fertilizing gametes and spontaneous abortion. Effect of th day of ovulation and the time of insemination," by R. Guerrero, ‹ al. AMER J OBSTET GYNEC 107:263-267, May 15, 1970.

"Control of fertility," by M. L. Peterson. NEW ENG J MED 282:14: 1433, June 18, 1970.

"Fertility control: health and educational factors for the 1970s. Con traception or abortion?" by J. H. Hughes. J BIOSOC SCI 2:161-166, April, 1970.

"Ideal means of fertility control?" by A. Gillespie, et al. LANCET 1:717, April 4, 1970.

"Prcstaglandins in fertility control," by S. M. Karim. LANCET 1:1 May 23, 1970.

FETUS

"A case of encephalocele in a fetus in pregnancy complicated by imminent abortion," by A. Lipinski, et al. WIAD LEK 23:1239-1241, July 15, 1970.

"Chromosomal anomalies in spontaneously aborted human fetuses,"' R. K. Dhadial, et al. LANCET 2:20-21, July 4, 1970.

"Fetal erythrocytes in maternal circulation after spontaneous aborti by O. Litwak, et al. JAMA 214:531-534, October 19, 1970.

"Fetal indications for termination of pregnancy," by H. L. Nadler. SEMIN PSYCHIAT 2,3:302-308, 1970.

"Feto-maternal haemorrhage at therapeutic abortion," by A. H. Johı et al. J OBSTET GYNAEC BRIT COMM 77:137-138, February, 1970.

"Fetuses and newborns of 95 per cent pancreatectomized female rat by V. G. Foglia. METAB DIS 1:Suppl 1:221+, 1970.

"The foetus began to cry ... abortion 1," by G. H. Green. NEW ZEAL NURS J 63:11-12, July, 1970; 2. 63:6-7, August, 1970; 3. 63:11-12, September, 1970.

"Infection of the fetus by Candida in a spontaneous abortion," by C. Y. Ho, et al. AMER J OBSTET GYNEC 106:705-710, March, 1970.

"The role of fetal death in the process of therapeutic abortion induced by intra-amniotic injection of hypertonic saline," by L. Kovacs, et al. J OBSTET GYNAECOL BR COMMONW 77:1132-1136, December, 1970.

"State of fetus in women with threatened abortion," by W. I. Griszczenko, ^t al. GINEK POL 41:19-21, January, 1970.

GENETICS

"Aberrant karyotypes and spontaneous abortion in a Japanese family," by T. Kadotani, et al. NATURE 225:735-737, February 21, 1970.

"Abortion caused by chromosomal abnormalities and estrogen insufficiency of the corpus luteum," by J. Cohen. PRESSE MED 78:1744, September 26, 1970.

"Abortion and genetic disorders," by V. G. Kirkels. NED TIJDSCHR VERLOSKD GYNAECOL 70:445-453, October, 1970.

"Anatomic and chromosomal anomalies in spontaneous abortion. Possible correlation with overripeness of oocytes," by K. Mikamo. AMER J OBSTET GYNEC 106:243-254, January 15, 1970.

"Chromosomal abnormalities and spontaneous abortion," MED J AUST 2:992-994, November 28, 1970.

"Chromosomal anomalies in spontaneously aborted human fetuses," by R. K. Dhadial, et al. LANCET 2:20-21, July 4, 1970.

"Chromosome aberrations in human spontaneous abortion," by J. G. Boué, et al. PRESSE MED 78:635-641, March 21, 1970.

"Chromosome aberrations in spontaneous abortion," by P. Dráč, et a CESK GYNEK 35:230-233, May, 1970 (42 ref.).

"Chromosome pathology in repeated abortions," by S. Rugiati, et al. MINERVA GINEC 22:81-86, January 31, 1970.

"Chromosome studies in selected spontaneous abortion. 1. Conceptio after oral contraceptives," by D. H. Carr. CANAD MED ASS J 10 343-348, August 15, 1970.

"Chromosomes and abortions," by S. L. Larson, et al. MAYO CLIN PROC 45:60-72, January, 1970 (65 ref.).

"Chromosomes in spontaneous abortions," by B. Padeh, et al. HAREFAUH 78:158-161, February 15, 1970.

"Cytogenetic aspects of habitual abortion. 2. Observation of satellite association in couples with history of habitual abortion," by K. Koike. NAGOYA MED J 16:72-79, November, 1970.

"Cytogenetic studies on mid-trimester abortuses," by P. Ruzicska, e al. HUMANGENETIK 10:273-297, 1970.

"Cytogenetics of spontaneous abortion. The chromosomes of decidua by D. T. Arakaki, et al. AMER J OBSTET GYNEC 107:1199-120 August 15, 1970.

"Estrogenic insufficiency and genetic abortions," by J. Cohen, et al BULL FED SOC GYNECOL OBSTET LANG FR 22:439-442, September-October, 1970.

"Inherited 13/14 chromosome translocation as a cause of human feta. wastage," by R. S. Sparkes, et al. OBSTET GYNEC 35:601-607, April, 1970.

"Morphological study of human embryos with chromosome aberrations by C. Roux. PRESSE MED 78:647-652, March 21, 1970.

"New biology and the prenatal child," by D. W. Brodie. J FAMILY L 9:391, 1970.

GENETICS

"Parental chromosomal aberrations associated with multiple abortions and an abnormal infant," by L. Y. Hsu, et al. OBSTET GYNECOL 36:723-730, November, 1970.

"Placenta and chromosome aberrations in spontaneous abortion," by E. Philippe, et al. PRESSE MED 78:641-646, March 21, 1970.

"Some effects of abnormal karyotype on intra-uterine growth and development," by D. I. Rushton. J PATHOL 101:Pxi, August, 1970.

"Survey on eugenics with special reference to public awareness," by T. Matsuura, et al. J JAP MED ASS 63:1516-1520, June 15, 1970.

GYNAECOLOGY

"Benzidamine and tetracycline therapy in gynecologic and obstetrical pathology," by L. Tinelli, et al. MINERVA GINECOL 22:677-680, July 15, 1970.

"Gynaecology in a permissive society," by T. L. Lewis. AUST NZ J OBSTET GYNAECOL 10:244-251, November, 1970.

"The gynecologist and therapeutic abortion: the changing times," by R. R. De Aluarez, et al. SEMIN PSYCHIAT 2,3:275-282, 1970.

"Oral administration of an association of an antibiotic, enzymes and balsam in septic inflammatory diseases in gynecology and obstetrics," by G. Locardi. MINERVA MED 61:961-965, March 10, 1970.

"Thiophenicol in current gynecological and obstetrical pathology," by M. Cathely. REV FR GYNECOL OBSTET 64:293-295, May, 1969.

HABITUAL ABORTION

"Chromosome pathology in repeated abortions," by S. Rugiati, et al. MINERVA GINEC 22:81-86, January 31, 1970.

"Cytogenetic aspects of habitual abortion. 2. Observation of satellite association in couples with history of habitual abortion," by K. Koike. NAGOYA MED J 16:72-79, November, 1970.

HABITUAL ABORTION

"Determinant factors in habitual abortion," by C. MacGregor, et al. GINEC OBSTET MEX 27:331-350, March, 1970.

"Differences in the submicroscopic structure of the epithelial cells o the secreting endometrium in healthy women and women with habit ual abortions," by M. Dvořák, et al. ZENTRALBL GYNAEKOL 9 1241-1248, September 19, 1970.

"Habitual abortion," by I. S. Rozovskii. MED SESTRA 29:29-32, February, 1970.

"Habitual abortion and premature labor caused by primary cervical insufficiency. Surgical and pharmacological treatment," by G. Colucci, et al. MINERVA GINECOL 21:687-688, May 31, 1969.

"Isthmic diseases and habitual abortion. Importance of isthmectomy," by F. Salvi. MINERVA GINECOL 21:679-681, May 31, 1969.

"Isthmus encircling by abdominal route, apart from pregnancy, with an aponeurosis band in habitual abortions," by J. Y. Gillet, et al. BULL FED GYNEC OBSTET FRANC 22:132-134, January-March, 1970.

"Prevention of hypothalamic habitual abortion by periactin," by E. Sadovsky, et al. HAREFUAH 78:332-334, April 1, 1970.

"Preventive cesarean section in women with habitual abortion," by J Kopečný, et al. CESK GYNEKOL 35:579-580, November, 1970.

"Psychological aspects of habitual abortion," by M. Silverman, et al PSYCHIATR COMMUN 13:35-43, 1970.

"Repeated or habitual abortions," Q MED REV 21:1-30, July, 1970 (61 ref.).

"Results of gestanon therapy in women with threatened and habitual abortion," by Ts. Despodova. AKUSH GINEKOL (Sofiia) 9:208-2 1970.

"Successful surgical management of uterine anomalies in habitual abortions," by A. Zwinger, et al. CESK GYNEK 35:275-277, 197

HEMORRHAGE
see also: Complications
         Transplacental Hemorrhage

"Administration of epsilon-aminocaproic acid (EACA) in the prevention of fibrinolytic hemorrhages associated with the expulsion of the fetus remaining in the uterus after its death," by E. Howorka, et al. WIAD LEK 23:973-977, June, 1970.

"Analysis of blood loss in artificial termination of pregnancy under local anesthesia," by J. Higier, et al. WAID LEK 23:1289-1293, August 1, 1970.

"Atonic hemorrhage in pregnancy interruption and its complications due to coagulation disorders," by O. Vago. ZBL GYNAEK 92:62-63, January 10, 1970.

"The effects of anesthesia and pulmonary ventilation on blood loss during elective therapeutic abortion," by B. F. Cullen, et al. ANESTHESIOLOGY 32:108-113, February, 1970.

"Feto-maternal haemorrhage at therapeutic abortion," by A. H. John, et al. J OBSTET GYNAEC BRIT COMM 77:137-138, February, 1970.

"Influence of ornithine 8-vasopressin preparation upon blood loss after induced abortions performed under local anesthesia," by J. Higier, et al. GINEK POL 41:731-734, July, 1970.

"Late hemorrhage following undetected uterine ruptures during pregnancy interruptions," by J. Andrŷs, et al. CESK GYNEK 35:364-365, July, 1970.

"Post-abortum hemorrhage caused by intravascula coagulation. Cure by Hysterectomy," by J. Testart, et al. ANN CHIR 24:229-234, February, 1970.

HISTORY
"Abortion reform: history, status, and prognosis," by W. Case. RES L REV 21:521, April, 1970.

HISTORY

"The abortion revolution," by R. Hall, M.D. PLAYBOY 17:112-114+, September, 1970.

"Panorama of abortion across the ages," by L. Fortier. UNION MED CAN 98:1534-1539, September, 1969.

HORMONES

"Attempted prevention of the embryotoxic and teratogenic effects of actinomycin D. II. Influence of the lactogenic hormone," by H. Tuchmann-Duplessis, et al. C R SOC BIOL 164:60-63, 1970.

"Clinical aspects of hormonal protection during pregnancy," by G. A Hauser. NED TIJDSCHR VERLOSKD GYNAECOL 70:436-445, October, 1970.

"Contractibility of the human uterus and the hormonal situation. Stud on therapy with progesterone in pregnancy," by P. Mentasti, et al MINERVA GINECOL 21:685-687, May 31, 1969.

"Cytohormonal studies of vaginal smears performed during the treatment of imminent abortions," by B. Wierstakow, et al. GINEKOL POL 41:977-984, September, 1970.

"High doses of progesterone in the therapy of hormonal abortion and the prevention of various types of pregnancy interruption," by C. Morra, et al. MINERVA GINECOL 21:699-701, May 31, 1969.

"High risk obstetrics. 3. Cytohormonal evaluations and their practice utility in managing high-risk patients," by R. H. Aubry, et al. AN J OBSTET GYNEC 107:48-64, May 1, 1970.

"Hormonal and vaginal cytology changes induced by a pregnane in threatened abortion," by J. Bravo Sandoval, et al. GINECOL OBSTET MEX 28:573-579, November, 1970.

"Hormonal problems of threatened early pregnancy," by M. Tausk. N TIJDSCHR VERLOSKD GYNAECOL 70:430-436, October, 1970.

"Hormone levels in threatened abortion," by J. B. Brown, et al. J OBSTET GYNAEC BRIT COMM 77:690-700, August, 1970.

"Prognostic value of urinary hormonal determinations during pregnancy," by P. Gellé, et al. REV FR GYNECOL OBSTET 64:215-233, May, 1969.

HOSPITALS & ABORTION

"Abortion and the hospital," by P. A. Richardson, et al. NEW YORK J MED 70:2144-2145, August 15, 1970.

"Abortion, the hospital and the law," by D. F. Phillips. HOSPITALS 44:59-62, August 16, 1970.

"Abortion goes public. Hospitals report 2,000 abortions in first week under new N.Y. law," MOD HOSP 115:33-36, August, 1970.

"1,229 cases of abortion in the Caldas University Hospital," by O. Vélez Ramirez. REV COLOMBIA OBSTET GINEC 21:147-170, March-April, 1970.

"Hospital abortion committee as an administrative body of the state," J FAMILY L 10:32, 1970.

"Physician attitudes toward hospital abortion in Georgia--1970," by G. Freeman, et al. J MED ASSOC GA 59:437-446, December, 1970.

"Preparing for abortion procedures," HOSPITALS 44:69, August 16, 1970.

INDUCED ABORTION
see also: Techniques of Abortion

"Analysis of blood loss in artificial termination of pregnancy under local anesthesia," by J. Higier, et al. WIAD LEK 23:1289-1293, August 1, 1970.

"Artificial abortion and immunization with antigens A or B in women with blood group O," by M. Jakubowska, et al. POL TYG LEK 25:1263-1264, August 17, 1970.

"Artificial pregnancy interruption and birth rate," by K. Vácha. CESK GYNEK 35:329-330, July, 1970.

INDUCED ABORTION

"Atonic hemorrhage in pregnancy interruption and its complications d
to coagulation disorders," by O. Vago. ZBL GYNAEK 92:62-63,
January 10, 1970.

"Combined use of the aspiration method and abortion forceps in induc
abortion between the 13th and 18th week of pregnancy," by A.
Atanasov, et al. AKUSH GINEKOL (Sofiia) 9:223-228, 1970.

"Critical study of mono and diphasic methods of artificial interruptio
of pregnancy," by W. Weise, et al. ZBL GYNAK 92,26:841-848,
1970.

"Effect of induced abortion on birth rate: a simulation model," by S.
Mukherji, et al. INDIAN J PUBLIC HEALTH 14:49-58, January,
1970.

"Effective surgical procedures for interruption of pregnancy in the
second trimester," by Y. Onishi. SANFUJIN JISSAI 19:73-78,
January, 1970.

"Evaluation of sequellae and possibilities of pregnancy interruption
by women who experienced it," by E. Dlhoš, et al. CESK GYNEK
35:336-338, July, 1970.

"Execution without trial," by A. W. Liley. NZ NURS J 63:6-7,
December, 1970.

"Experience in anesthesia for artificial interrupting of pregnancy by
new intravenous anesthetic, propanidid (Epontol)," by K. Nagauc
et al. SANFUJIN JISSAI 19:873-876, August, 1970.

"Hazards of 1st pregnancy interruptions," by L. Sokolik, et al. CESK
GYNEK 35:373-374, July, 1970.

"High doses of progesterone in the therapy of hormonal abortion and
the prevention of various types of pregnancy interruption," by C.
Morra, et al. MINERVA GINECOL 21:699-701, May 31, 1969.

"Hysterographic changes following uterine injury during artificial int
ruption of pregnancy," by V. Nesit. CESK GYNEK 35:353-354,
July, 1970.

INDUCED ABORTION

"The hysterosalpingographic picture following interruption of the 1st pregnancy," by L. Láska, et al. CESK GYNEK 35:352-353, July, 1970.

"Induced abortion and its consequences," by S. Sasu, MUNCA SANIT 18:157-160, March, 1970.

"Induced abortion in Lebanon," by W. M. Bickers. J MED LIBAN 23: 467:470, 1970.

"Induced abortion in the Maternal-Child Institute," by L. E. Santamariá Páez. REV COLOMBIA OBSTET GINEC 21:137-139, March-April, 1970.

"Induced abortion in a municipal hospital," by H. Schulman. OBSTET GYNECOL 36:616-620, October, 1970.

"Induction of abortion by prostaglandins E1 and E2," by M. P. Embrey. BRIT MED J 1:258-260, May 2, 1970.

"Induction of abortion using high doses of oxytocin," by J. Kopečný, et al. CESK GYNEK 35:118-119, March, 1970.

"Induction of therapeutic abortion with intravenous prostaglandin," by F. Wiqvist, et al. LANCET 1:889, April 25, 1970.

"Inflammation of genitalia following artificial pregnancy interruption," by J. Diviš, et al. CESK GYNEK 35:371-372, July, 1970.

"Influence of 1st pregnancy interruption on later gestation," by P. Heczko, et al. CESK GYNEK 35:333-334, July, 1970.

"Influence of ornithine 8-vasopressin preparation upon blood loss after induced abortions performed under local anesthesia," by J. Higier, et al. GINEK POL 41:731-734, July, 1970.

"Insertion of IUD following artificial abortion," by J. Koukal, et al. CESK GYNEKOL 35:465-467, October, 1970.

"Interruption graviditatis and lysis manualis placentae," by V. Brutar, et al. CESK GYNEK 35:335-336, July, 1970.

69

"Interruption of late term pregnancy by means of vaginal cesarean section," by Z. Ia. Gendon. AKUSH GINEK 46:58-61, January, 1970.

"Interruption of pregnancy before the period of fetal viability. The opinion of the national medical council about the abortion," PRES MED 78:2147-2149, November 14, 1970.

"Is pregnancy interruption necessary following failure of the intra-uterine device (IUD)," by M. Kohoutek, et al. CESK GYNEK 35:3 342, July, 1970.

"Kovacs' semiconservative method of pregnancy interruption," by I. Vido, et al. CESK GYNEK 35:345-347, July, 1970.

"Late hemorrhage following undetected uterine ruptures during pregna cy interruptions," by J. Andrýs, et al. CESK GYNEK 35:364-365, July, 1970.

"Long-term follow up of secondary sterility following artificial inter-ruption of pregnancy," by O. Kolářová. CESK GYNEKOL 35:399-400, September, 1970.

"Macroscopic changes in the placenta after numerous induced abor-tions," by B. Kh. Aronov. AKUSH GINEKOL 46:72-73, July, 197

"Menstruation disorders following artificial interruption of pregnancy by F. Macků, et al. CESK GYNEKOL 35:401-402, September, 197

"Mental and sexual problems related to pregnancy interruption," by C Kolářová. CESK GYNEK 35:378-379, July, 1970.

"Most frequent complications of artificial pregnancy interruption with 10 years," by K. Zák. CESK GYNEK 35:367-368, July, 1970.

"Observation of tissue antibodies in artificial pregnancy interruption by A. Kotásek, et al. CESK GYNEK 35:356-357, July, 1970.

"Occurrence of ectopic pregnancy following artificial abortion," by Macků, et al. CESK GYNEK 35:375-377, July, 1970.

"Our experience with anesthesia in artificial pregnancy interruption," by K. Hrazdil. CESK GYNEK 35:349-350, July, 1970.

"Our experience with the IUD (contraceptive loop) inserted immediately after interruption of pregnancy," by Z. Szereday, et al. ORV HETIL 111:2299-2300, September 27, 1970.

"Placental acetylcholine in induction of premature labor," by R. C. Goodlin. AMER J OBSTET GYNEC 107:429-431, June 1, 1970.

"Plasma progesterone levels during bougie-induced abortion in mid-pregnancy," by Y. Manabe. J ENDOCR 46:127-128, January, 1970.

"Plasma progesterone levels during saline-induced abortion," by W. G. Wiest, et al. J CLIN ENDOCR 30:774-777, June, 1970.

"Possible isoimmunization following legal interruption of pregnancy," by A. Pontuch, et al. CESK GYNEK 35:357-358, July, 1970.

"Pregnancy interruption by means of vibrodilation and vacuum aspiration," by J. Német, et al. ZBL GYNAEK 92:120-127, January 24, 1970.

"Premature termination of pregnancy following previous artificial interruption of pregnancy," by P. Dráč, et al. CESK GYNEK 35:332-333, July, 1970.

"Primary indication of surgical pregnancy interruption," by M. Chalupa, et al. CESK GYNEK 35:344-345, July, 1970.

"Prostaglandins and the induction of labour or abortion," LANCET 1: 927-928, May 2, 1970.

"Quantitative changes in plasmaa fibrinogen in women prepared for pregnancy interruption by intravenous injection of EACA," by E. Howorka, et al. PRZEGL LEK 26:378-390, March 18, 1970.

"The relationship between progesterone, uterine volume, intrauterine pressure, and clinical progress in hypertonic saline--induced abortions," by A. I. Csapo, et al. AM J OBSTET GYNECOL 108: 950-955, November 15, 1970.

INDUCED ABORTION

"Rotilan anesthesia in induced abortion," by I. A. Vainberg, et al. AKUSH GINEKOL 46:73, July, 1970.

"Scientific organization of the work of medical personnel in surger for the interruption of early pregnancy," by A. A. Bagrov, et al AKUSH GINEKOL 46:69-70, November, 1970.

"Sequelae of artificial interruption of pregnancy in juveniles," by Mandausová, et al. CESK GYNEKOL 35:402-404, September, 1

"Sequellae of artificial pregnancy interruption," by J. Houdek, et a CESK GYNEK 35:368-369, July, 1970.

"Sequellae of artificial pregnancy interruption," by A. Kotásek. CESK GYNEK 35:325-328, July, 1970.

"Sequellae of artificial pregnancy interruption," by V. Skála. CES GYNEK 35:370-371, July, 1970.

"Sex disorders following artificial pregnancy interruption," by F. Kohoutek, et al. CESK GYNEK 35:380-381, July, 1970.

"Sex ratio in human embryos obtained from induced abortion: histo ical examination of the gonad in 1,452 cases," by S. Lee, et a AM J OBSTET GYNECOL 108:1294-1297, December 15, 1970.

"The share of complications of artificial pregnancy interruption in hospital morbidity," by V. Laně, et al. CESK GYNEK 35:374-: July, 1970.

"Significance of abortion and pregnancy interruption for the passag fetal erythrocytes and anti Rh (D) antibody formation," by Z. Křikal, et al. CESK GYNEK 35:359-360, July, 1970.

"Significance of sterility following artificial interruption of pregna by M. Kohoutek, et al. CESK GYNEKOL 35:398-399, Septembe 1970.

"Spontaneous and induced abortion. Report of a WHO scientific group WHO TECH REP SER 461:3-51, 1970.

"Sterility following artificial interruption of 1st pregnancy," by K. Jirátko, et al. CESK GYNEKOL 35:397-398, September, 1970.

"Surveillance of women following rejection of their application for artificial pregnancy interruption," by M. Zdímalová, et al. CESK GYNEK 35:338-340, July, 1970.

"Techniques of abortion," by W. J. Cameron. J KANS MED SOC 71: 375-377, October, 1970.

"Threatened pregnancies," by Gregoire. BULL SOC SCI MED GRAND DUCHE LUXEMB 107:277-286, October, 1970.

"Unusual case of intestinal lesions after induced abortion. Accidental finding in extragenital pathology," by F. Peretti. MINERVA GINEC 22:252-255, February 28, 1970.

"Use of a combination of an antibiotic with proteolytic enzymes in post-abortion pelvic infection," by E. Acosta Bendek. GINEC OBSTET MEX 27:297-305, March, 1970.

"The uterine cervix following artificial pregnancy interruption," by K. Sapák, et al. CESK GYNEK 35:355-356, July, 1970.

"Uterus injury in artificial pregnancy interruption and its sequellae," by V. Nesit. CESK GYNEK 35:360-362, July, 1970.

"Uterus perforation as a complication of legal pregnancy interruption," by R. Kronus, et al. CESK GYNEK 35:362-364, July, 1970.

"Work of the commission for pregnancy interruption in Berlin," by L. Waldeyer. DEUTSCH GESUNDH 25:28-32, January 9, 1970.

NFECTION
see: Complications

UD
see: Contraception

LABOR
"Blood circulation and temperature of the uterus in a normal pregna and in threatened premature labor," by T. A. Serova, et al. VOF OKHR MATERIN DET 15:71-74, November, 1970.

"Course and outcome of labor after threatened abortion," by H. Wal et al. GEBURTSHILFE FRAUENHEILKD 30:504-513, June, 19

"Endonasal electrophoresis in the treatment of premature labor," b I. Bodiazhina, et al. AKUSH GINEK 46:58-65, April, 1970.

"Hysterography in intrauterine pregnancy and abortion. Report of th cases," by M. Honoré. ACTA RADIOL 10:489-493, November, 1970.

"Outcome of labor for the mother and child after pregnancy complica by threatened abortion," by L. V. Ananich. VOPR OKHR MATE DET 15:68-71, November, 1970.

"Placental acetylcholine in induction of premature labor," by R. C Goodlin. AMER J OBSTET GYNEC 107:429,431, June 1, 1970.

"Pregnancy and labor in women with isthmic-cervical insufficiency by S. A. Galitskaia, et al. PEDIATR AKUSH GINEKOL 4:43-4! July-August, 1970.

LAW ENFORCEMENT
"Abortion on request; Hawaii," TIME 95:34, March 9, 1970.

"Abortion on request: Its consequences for population trends and public health," by C. Tietze. SEMIN PSYCHIAT 2,3:375-381, 1

"Abortion request and post-operative response. A Washington comm survey," by R. J. Pion, et al. NORTHWEST MED 69:693-698, . tember, 1970.

"Abortion and sterilization. Status of the law in mid-1970," by N. Hershey. AMER J NURS 70:1926-1927, September, 1970.

"Attempt at abortion with potassium permanganate tablets," by A. Le Coz, et al. BULL FED SOC GYNECOL OBSTET LANG FR

20:190-191, April-May, 1968.

"Comparative epidemiologic study between patients with and without previous illegal abortions," by F. J. Zozaya, et al. GINEC OBSTET MEX 27:147-182, February, 1970.

"The consequences of criminal abortion on the woman's state of health," by M. Handru. MUNCA SANIT 18:345-348, June, 1970.

"Constitutional law-criminal abortion-statute prohibiting intentional destruction of unquickened fetus violates mother's right of privacy," GA L REV 4:907, Summer, 1970.

"Constitutional law-criminal law-requirement of certainty in legislation in a criminal abortion statute," J URBAN L 47:901, 1969-1970.

"Crime of abortion; address, April 9, 1970," by B. F. Brown. VITAL SPEECHES 36:549-553, July 1, 1970.

"Criminal law-abortion-man, being without a legal beginning," KY L J 58:843, Summer, 1969-1970.

"Criminal law-abortion statute-due process-the supreme court of California has held that a statute prohibiting abortions not "necessary to preserve" the mother's life is so vague and uncertain as to be violative to the fourteenth amendment's due process clause," DUQUESNE L REV 8:439, Summer, 1970.

"Criminal procedure-search and seizure-electronic eavesdropping-abortion: recording of voluntary conversation between police agent and defendant admissible in evidence," WASH L REV 45:411, April, 1970.

"Death following criminal abortion with hypertonic saline," by G. Weiss. NEW YORK J MED 70:312-315, January 15, 1970.

"Feticide infanticide upon request," by P. Ramsey. RELIGION IN LIFE 39:170-186, Summer, 1970.

"The influence of medical and biological progress: the contemporary criminal law of abortion," by D. Bein. in Feller, S. Z., ed.

ISRAELI REPORTS TO THE EIGHTH INTERNATIONAL CON-
GRESS OF COMPARATIVE LAW, 1970, 196-203.

"Natural law institute 1970: abortion. Recent statutes and the crime
of abortion," by B. F. Brown; "Abortion: a human problem," by
W. J. Kenealy; "Abortion: a moral or medical problem?" by L.
Salzman. LOYOLA L REV 16:275, 1969-1970.

"New Mexico's 1969 criminal abortion law," by J. B. Sutin. NATU-
RAL RESOURCES J 10:591, July, 1970.

"Pregnancy outcome of women whose application for pregnancy inter
ruption had been rejected," by M. Kohoutek, et al. CESK GYNEK
35:340-341, July, 1970.

"Problems in enforcement of the abortion law," by T. Matsuura. J JA
MED ASSOC 64:1191-1194, November 15, 1970.

"Right of action for injury to, or death of a woman who consented to
abortion," by D. Evans. J MED ASSOC STATE ALA 40:334 pas
November, 1970

"Right not to be born; refusal to grant therapeutic abortion in case o
rubella baby," by M. K. Sanders. HARPER 240:92-99, April, 197

"Surveillance of women following rejection of their application for
artificial pregnancy interruption," by M. Zdímalová, et al. CESK
GYNEK 35:338-340, July, 1970.

"Therapeutic abortion--Washington, D.C.," by E. J. Connor, et al.
MED AM DC 39:133-137 passim, March, 1970.

LAWS & LEGISLATION

"Abortion act," by J. P. Crawford. LANCET 2:1138, November 28,
1970.

"The abortion act: a general practitioner's view," by J. McEwan.
PRACTITIONER 204:427-432, March, 1970.

"Abortion act in action," by C. B. Goodhart. NATURE 227:757-758, August 15, 1970.

"The Abortion Act 1967. (a). The advantages and disadvantages," by D. Baird. R SOC HEALTH J 90:291-295, November- December, 1970.

"The Abortion Act (1967). Findings of an inquiry into the first year's working of the Act conducted by the Royal College of Obstetricians and Gynaecologists," BRIT MED J 2:529-535, May 30, 1970.

"Abortion and the birth rate in the USSR," by G. Hyde. J BIOSOC SCI 2:283-292, July, 1970.

"Abortion and the changing law," NEWSWEEK 75:53-56+, April 13, 1970.

"Abortion and the constitutional question," SD L REV 15:318, Spring, 1970.

"Abortion and the courts," SCIENTIFIC AMERICAN 222:50+, January, 1970.

"Abortion and the law: anachronisms racing science," J MISSISSIPPI MED ASS 11:335-336, June, 1970.

"Abortion and legal rationality," by J. Finnis. ADELAIDE L REV 3:431, August, 1970.

"Abortion and responsibility," AMERICAN 122:400, April 18, 1970.

"Abortion: condescension or prevention," by B. McKie. MED J AUST 1:821, April 18, 1970.

"Abortion. Condescension or prevention," by R. S. Wurm. MED J AUST 1:557-562, March 14, 1970.

"Abortion-constitutional law-a law that allows an abortion only when "necessary to preserve" the life of the mother violates a qualified constitutional right to an abortion and is unconstitutionally vague," TEX L REV 48:937, May, 1970.

"Abortion counseling in legal trouble: Rabbi Ticktin on conspiracy charges," CHR CENT 87:68, January 21, 1970.

"Abortion debate," COMMONWEAL 92:131-132, April 24, 1970,

"Abortion, the hospital and the law," by D. F. Phillips. HOSPITAL 44:59-62, August 16, 1970.

"Abortion in America," by H. Rosen. AMER J PSYCHIAT 126:1299-1301, March, 1970.

"The abortion controversy," by E. B. Smith. J NATL MED ASSOC 6 379, September, 1970.

"Abortion in court," ECONOMIST 234:48, February 28, 1970.

"Abortion in New York," NEWSWEEK 76:52, October 5, 1970.

"Abortion in New York," TIME 96:48, September 7, 1970.

"The abortion issue," by H. Teilmann. T SYGEPL 70:10-11, Janua 1970.

"Abortion Law," NEW STATESMAN 80:138, August 7, 1970.

"Abortion Law," NEW STATESMAN 80:786, December 11, 1970.

"Abortion law-California abortion law voided," DICK L REV 74:77: Summer, 1970.

"Abortion: law, ethics and the value of life," by C. Burke. MANCH MED GAZ 49:4-9, July, 1970.

"Abortion law in Massachusetts," by M. L. Taymor. NEW ENG J ME 283:602, September 10, 1970.

"Abortion law reform," by Richard L. Worsnop. EDITORIAL RE-SEARCH REPTS p. 545-562, July 24, 1970.

"Abortion law reform: how the controversy changed," by M. Simms. CRIM L R 1970:567, October, 1970.

"Abortion law reform progress in Michigan," by J. M. Stack. MICH MED 69:23-27, January, 1970.

"Abortion laws: an appeal for repeal (proposes repeal (not reform) of all laws relating to abortion except those governing the practice of medicine generally)," by G. Clyde Dodder. RIPON FORUM 6:20-22, May, 1970.

"Abortion laws: a commentary," by Neil Snortland. YOUR GOVT 25:3-4, March 15, 1970.

"Abortion laws. Constitutional questions," by A. R. Holder. JAMA 214:2405-2406, December 28, 1970.

"Abortion laws: a study in social change," by T. G. Moyers. SAN DIEGO L REV 7:237, May, 1970.

"Abortion laws, under challenge, are being liberalized (United States)," CONG Q W REPT 28:1913-1916, July 24, 1970.

"Abortion: a legal view," by N. W. Williamson. NZ MED J 72:257-261, October, 1970.

"Abortion legislation: a fundamental challenge," by L. Massett. SCI N 97:75-76, January 17, 1970.

"Abortion made easier," CHR TODAY 14:36, March 27, 1970.

"Abortion: new and old issues," AMERICA 122:666-667, June 27, 1970.

"Abortion: the new civil right," by E. Truninger. WOMEN LAW 56:86, Summer, 1970.

"Abortion on demand," by J. A. Fitzgerald. MED OPINION & REV 6: 110+, January, 1970.

"Abortion on demand: New York and Hawaii," TIME 96:34, July 6, 1970.

"Abortion-on-demand: whose morality?" by R. M. Byrn. NOTRE DAME LAW 46:5, Fall, 1970.

"Abortion, Oregon style," ORE L REV 49:302, April, 1970.

"Abortion reform," TIME 95:46, April 20, 1970.

"Abortion reform: history, status, and prognosis," by W. Case. RES L REV 21:521, April, 1970.

"Abortion reform: the new tokenism," by L. Cisler. RAMPARTS 9:19-25, August, 1970.

"Abortion: a startling proposal," by M. J. Halberstam. REDBOOK 134: 78-79+, April, 1970.

"Abortion under the new Colorado law," by S. W. Downing, et al. NEBRASKA MED J 55:24-30, January, 1970.

"Abortion veto; legislation vetoed by Maryland's Governor Marvin Mandel," NEW REPUB 162:8, June 13, 1970.

"Abortions on demand," NEWSWEEK 76:60, July 13, 1970.

"Abortions under the N.H.S.," by H. G. Arthure. BR MED J 4:617, December 5, 1970.

"Abortus provocatus, ethics and legislation," by A. Strom. T NORSK LAEGEFOREN 90:685-687, April 1, 1970.

"Action of privy Council on appeals from G.M.C.," BRIT MED J 1: 292, August 1, 1970.

"After abortion reform," AMERICA 122:449, April 25, 1970.

"After July 1, an abortion should be as simple to have as a tonsillec-tomy, but--," by L. Greenhouse. N Y TIMES MAG p7+, June 28, 1970.

"Are state abortion statutes reasonable?-- the recent judicial trend in-dicates the contrary," S T L J 11:426, 1970.

"Birth control and abortions legal battles past and present. Summary of paper given at annual meeting November 5-8, 1969," by H. Pilpel. WOM PHYCH 25,7:435-436, 1970.

"Britain's abortion act: inquiry requested," by T. Beeson. CHR CENT 87:984-985, August 19, 1970.

"A case for abortion and unrestrictive laws," by B. E. Fisher. THE NEW YORK LAW JOURNAL 164:1+, September 24, 1970.

"Certification of rape under the Colorado abortion statute," U COLO L REV 42:121, May, 1970.

"Change the abortion law now; editorial," by D. Anderson. CHATE-LAINE 43:1, Summer, 1970.

"Colorado's abortion law: an obstetrician's view," by C. Dafoe NEBRASKA MED J 55:3-4, January, 1970.

"The Colorado report," by A. Heller, et al. SEMIN PSYCHIAT 2,3:361-374, 1970.

"Constitutional law-abortion-1850 California statute prohibiting all abortions not "necessary to preserve (the mother's) life" is unconstitutionally vague and an improper infringement on women's constitutional rights," NOTRE DAME LAW 45:329, Winter, 1970.

"Constitutional law-abortion-does a woman have a constitutional right under the ninth amendment to choose whether to bear a child after conception," TEX TECH L REV 2:99, Fall, 1970.

"Constitutional law-abortion-standard excepting abortions done as "necessary for the preservation of the mother's life or health" held unconstitutionally vague," VAND L REV 23:821, May, 1970.

"Constitutional law-abortion-statute prohibiting abortion of unquickened fetus violates mother's constitutional right of privacy," VAND L REV 23:1346, November, 1970.

"Constitutional law-criminal abortion-statute prohibiting intentional destruction of unquickened fetus violates mother's right of privacy," GA L REV 4:907, Summer, 1970.

"Constitutional law-criminal law-requirement of certainty in legislation in a criminal abortion statute," J URBAN L 47:901, 1969-1970.

"Constitutional law-state regulation of abortion," WIS L REV 1970: 933, 1970.

"Constitutional law--void-for-vagueness," SUFFOLK U L REV 4:920, Spring, 1970.

"Constitutional question: is there a right to abortion?" by L. J. Greenhouse. N Y TIMES MAG p30-1+, January 25, 1970; Discussion p14+, February 22, 1970.

"Constitutional reflections on abortion reform," by P. L. Baude. JOURNAL OF LAW REFORM 4:1-10, Fall, 1970.

"Counseling and referral for legal abortion in California's (San Francisco) bay area," by Sadja Goldsmith, et al. FAMILY PLANNING PERSPECTIVES 2:14-19, June, 1970.

"Current status of abortion and premature births in cities," KANGO 22:117-122, May, 1970.

"Debates on abortion in United States," PRESSE MED 78:1899-1900, October 17, 1970.

"Easier abortion," SCI AM 222:47-48, June, 1970.

"Experience at Duke Medical Center after modern legislation for therapeutic abortion," by A. C. Christakos. SOUTHERN MED J 63:655-657, June, 1970.

"Extended birth control: Abortion on request," by J. G. Howells. CAN MENT HLTH 18:3+, September-October, 1970.

"Failure to advise: a basis for malpractice under the revised Oregon abortion act," WILLAMETTE L J 6:349, June, 1970.

"Fathers and sons: liberalization of New York state law," NEWSWEEK 75:77, April 20, 1970.

"1st liberalization of the abortion legislation in USA," by J. Padovec. CESK GYNEK 35:381, July, 1970.

"Gaines v. Wolcott (Ga) 167 S E 2d 366," MERCER L REV 21:325, Winter, 1970.

"Georgia Abortion Law unconstitutional," by J. L. Moore, Jr. J MED ASSOC GA 59:402-407, October, 1970.

"Guidelines for action about the New York abortion law," SOCIAL JUSTICE REVIEW 63:266-273, December, 1970.

"The impact of the Abortion Act 1967 in Great Britain," by P. H. Addison. MEDICOLEG J 38:15-21, 1970.

"I'm married, happy and went through hell for a legal abortion," by R. Squire. MACL MAG 83:51-52, 54-56, October, 1970.

"Mr. Irvine's bill," LANCET 1:343-344, February 14, 1970.

"Isolating the male bias against reform of abortion legislation," SANTA CLARA LAW 10:301, Spring, 1970.

"Japan wants to tighten its abortion law," MUNCHEN MED WSCHR 29:2, July 17, 1970.

"Jet-service abortion," by J. Dingman. CHATELAINE 43:4, June, 1970.

"Law, preventive psychiatry, and therapeutic abortion," by H. I. Levene, et al. J NERV MENT DIS 151:51-59, July, 1970.

"Legal abortion," by K. Soiva. DUODECIM 86:1295-1297, 1970.

"Legal abortion. On handling it in antenatal institutions and hospitalization problems with commentary on development of new abortion laws," by M. Landgreen. UGESKR LAEG 132:347-353, February 12, 1970.

"Legal abortion and medical ethics," by L. Ribeiro. HOSPITAL 78: 439-476, August, 1970.

"Legal abortion and social class," by W. H. James. LANCET 2:658, September 26, 1970.

"Legal abortion without hospitalization," by A. J. Margolis, et al. OBSTET GYNEC 36:479-481, September, 1970.

"Legal abortions at the Stockholm General Maternity Hospital in 1967-1968," by J. Abolins, et al. LAKARTIDNINGEN 67:4039-4045, September 2, 1970.

"Legal abortions in Norway 1965-1969," by B. Grünfeld, et al. T NORSK LAEGEFOREN 90:1261-1266, June 15, 1970.

"Legalized abortion: murder or mercy?" IMPRINT 17:12, January, 1970.

"Liberal abortion law, effective today, stirs worries in New York (N. Y.): doctors, hospitals fear they will be overwhelmed," by Peggy J. Murrell. WALL ST J 176:1+, July 1, 1970.

"National guide to legal abortion," by L. Lader. LADIES HOME J 87: 73, July, 1970.

"The new Abortion Act," T SYGEPL 70:218, May, 1970.

"The new abortion laws: How are they working?" by T. Irwin. TODAY HLTH 48:21+, March, 1970.

"New problems and old ones back again," LANCET 2:872-873, October 24, 1970.

"Up for approval," LANCET 1:760-761, April 11, 1970.

"People v. Belous (Cal) 458 P 2d 194," FORDHAM L REV 38:557, March, 1970; HARV CIVIL RIGHTS L REV 5:133, January, 1970; ND L REV 46:249, Winter, 1970; TEMP L Q 43:302, Spring, 1970; U RICHMOND L REV 4:351, Spring, 1970; WASH U L Q 1969:445

Fall, 1969; WASHBURN L J 9:286, Winter, 1970.

"Physicians' attitudes on the abortion law. Report of survey, 1969," by R. G. Smith, et al. HAWAII MED J 29:209-211, January-February, 1970.

"Preliminary assessment of the 1967 Abortion Act in practice," by P. Diggory, et al. LANCET 1:287-291, February 7, 1970.

"The present status of abortion laws: A statement by the New York Academy of Medicine prepared by the Committee on Public Health," BULL NY ACAD MED 46:281-285, April, 1970.

"The position of the Conseil de l'Ordre on some current problems," by J. Bréhant. PRESSE MED 78:1522-1523, July 11, 1970.

"Psychiatric experience with a liberalized therapeutic abortion law," by L. Marder. AMER J PSYCHIAT 126:1230-1236, March, 1970.

"Reforming the abortion laws: a doctor looks at the case," by D. Cavanagh. AMERICA 122:406-411, April 18, 1970; Discussion 122: 571, May 30, 1970.

"Reviewing the Abortion Act," by P. Draper. BRIT MED J 3:344, August 8, 1970.

"RSH Congress. The Abortion Act 1967 discussed," NURS MIRROR 130:13-15, June 26, 1970.

"Rubella and abortion laws," by W. A. Burns. MED LEG BULL 208: 1-7, August, 1970.

"Should abortion laws be liberalized? interviews," ed. by C. Remsberg, et al. GOOD H 170:92-93+, March, 1970.

"Should the United States legalize abortions? Yes," by B. Packwood; "No," by J. R. Rarick. AMERICAN LEGION MAGAZINE 88:22-23, June, 1970.

"Statement on implementation of the New York State abortion law by the Committee on Public Health of the New York Academy of Medicine. BULL NY ACAD MED 46:674-675, September, 1970.

"The Swedish abortion law and its application," by R. Lindelius. LAKARTIDNINGEN 67:5509-5519, November 18, 1970.

"Therapeutic abortion in a Canadian City," by R. M. Boyce, et al. CAN MED ASSOC J 103:461-466, September 12, 1970.

"Therapeutic abortion in Great Britain," by D. A. Pond. SEMIN PSYCHIAT 2,3:336-340, 1970.

"To be or not to be: the constitutional question of the California abortion law," U PA L REV 118:643, February, 1970.

"Tubal ligation and abortion in the State of Alabama," by C. E. Flowers, Jr. J MED ASS ALABAMA 39:945-947, April, 1970.

"Various problems involving the abortion law. Evaluation of the result of the study of its practice," by T. Yoshikawa. JAP J MIDWIFE 24:31-34, December, 1970.

"Veto for abortion; Maryland," NEWSWEEK 75:51-52, June 8, 1970.

"Washington abortion reform," GONZAGA L REV 5:270, Spring, 1970.

"When abortion is made easier: more and more states are discovering what happens when abortion laws are relaxed; demand is rising to make such operations, by licensed physicians, more available; eve a national law is proposed," U S NEWS 68:83, June 8, 1970.

LISTERIOSIS
"Listeriosis as cause of abortion," by R. Lange, et al. ZENTRALBL GYNAEKOL 92:313-318, March 7, 1970.

MALE ATTITUDES
see: Sociology

METACIN
"Evaluation of the effectiveness of metacin therapy in threatened premature labor and last abortion (clinico-hysterographic study)," by M. Ia. Martynshin. AKUSH GINEK 46:39-43, January, 1970.

MICROBIOLOGY
"Attempts to isolate H-1 virus from spontaneous human abortions: a negative report," by S. J. Newman, et al. TERATOLOGY 3:279-281, August, 1970.

"Differences in the submicroscopic structure of the epithelial cells of the secreting endometrium in healthy women and women with habitual abortions," by M. Dvořák, et al. ZENTRALBL GYNAEKOL 92:1241-1248, September 19, 1970.

"Microbial findings in isthmus and cervix insufficiency and their significance for the therapeutic result of cerclage (preliminary report)," by I. Penev, et al. AKUSH GINEKOL (Sofiia) 9:94-100, 1970.

MENSTRUATION
see: Complications
Induced Abortion

MISCARRIAGE
"Evaluation of results of surgical treatment of cervical isthmus insufficiency being the cause of late abortions and miscarriages," by W. Kokoszka, et al. PRZEGL LEK 26:769-770, 1970.

"Problems of miscarriage," by K. Niemineva. KATILOLEHTI 75:198-202, May, 1970.

"Use of mechanohysterography in the diagnosis of threatened miscarriage in women's consultation centers," by I. M. Griaznova, et al. VOP OKHR MATERIN DETS 15:64-67, February, 1970.

MORBIDITY
"The immediate morbidity of therapeutic abortion," by M. A. Carlton, et al. MED J AUST 2:1071-1074, December 5, 1970.

"The share of complications of artificial pregnancy interruption in

hospital morbidity," by V. Lanĕ, et al. CESK GYNEK 35:374-37
July, 1970.

MORTALITY
see also: Post Abortum Complications
Sepsis
Septic Abortion & Septic Shock

"Death following criminal abortion with hypertonic saline," by G.
Weiss. NEW YORK J MED 70:312-315, January 15, 1970.

"Maternal deaths due to sepsis with septic shock," OHIO MED J 66
589-591, June, 1970.

"Maternal mortality," J KENTUCKY MED ASS 68:416, July, 1970.

MYCOPLASMA
"Mycoplasma hominis and abortion," by H. J. Harwick, et al.
J INFECT DIS 121:260-268, March, 1970.

"The role of mycoplasmas in human reproductive failure," by R. B.
Kundsin, et al. ANN NY ACAD SCI 174:794-797, October 30, 19

NURSES & ABORTION
"The RN panel of 500 tells what nurses think about abortion," RN :
40-43, June, 1970.

"Surgical nursing: Abortions and sterilizations," REGAN REP NUR
LAW 11:1, June, 1970.

OBSTETRICS
"Assessment of the obstetric application of 17-hydroxyprogesterone
capronate (Hormofort)," by S. Němeti, et al. ORV HETIL 111:14
1407, June 14, 1970.

"Bacteremia shock syndrome in obstetrics," by I. Szemesi, et al.
ACTA CHIR ACAD SCI HUNG 11:87-95, 1970.

"Benzidamine and tetracycline therapy in gynecologic and obstetrica
pathology," by L. Tinelli, et al. MINERVA GINECOL 22:677-68
July 15, 1970.

"Future perspectives of prenatal pediatrics," by C. Haffter. ACTA PAEDOPSYCHIATR 37:241-243, December, 1970.

"High-risk obstetrics. 3. Cytohormonal evaluations and their practical utility in managing high-risk patients," by R. H. Aubry, et al. AMER J OBSTET GYNEC 107:48-64, May 1, 1970.

"Oestrogen and pregnanediol excretion in various obstetrical populations," by J. B. Brown, et al. PROC R SOC MED 63:1092-1095, November, 1970.

"Oral administration of an association of an antibiotic, enzymes and balsam in septic inflammatory diseases in gynecology and obstetrics," by G. Locardi. MINERVA MED 61:961-965, March 10, 1970.

OXYTOCIN
"The effect of oxytocin on the complication rate of early therapeutic abortions," by E. D. B. Johansson. ACTA OBSTET GYNEC SCAND 49,2:129-131, 1970.

"Induction of abortion using high doses of oxytocin," by J. Kopečný, et al. CESK GYNEK 35:118-119, March, 1970.

PERIACTIN
"Prevention of hypothalamic habitual abortion by periactin," by E. Sadovsky, et al. HAREFUAH 78:332-334, April 1, 1970.

PHYSICIANS & ABORTIONS
see *also*: Sociology

"Abortion. Should the physician be the conscience of society?" by E. B. Linton, et al. OBSTET GYNEC 35:465-467, March, 1970.

"The abortion act: a general practitioner's view," by J. McEwan. PRACTITIONER 204:427-432, March, 1970.

"Abortion: due process and the doctor's dilemma," J FAMILY L 9:300, 1970.

"Abortion: The medical and psychological view," by J. E. Brody. WOMAN'S DAY 34:68+, October, 1970.

"Abortion: a physician's view," by W. R. Roy. WASHBURN L J 9:3 Spring, 1970.

"Abortion or no? What decides? An inquiry by questionnaire into the attitudes of gynecologists and psychiatrists in Aberdeen," by C. McCance, et al. SEMIN PSYCHIAT 2,3:352-360, 1970.

"Colorado's abortion law: an obstetrician's view," by C. Dafoe. NEBRASKA MED J 55:3-4, January, 1970.

"Consultants' report on abortion," BRIT MED J 2:491-492, May 30, 1970.

"General practitioners' views on pregnancy termination," by W. Sussman, et al. MED J AUST 2:169-173, July 25, 1970.

"How doctors perform abortions," by D. R. Zimmerman. LADIES HO J 87:38+, November, 1970.

"Interruption of pregnancy before the period of fetal viability. The opinion of the national medical council about the abortion," PRESSE MED 78:2147-2149, November 14, 1970.

"Legal abortion and medical ethics," by L. Ribeiro. HOSPITAL 78 439-476, August, 1970.

"Physician attitudes toward hospital abortion in Georgia--1970," by G. Freeman, et al. J MED ASSOC GA 59:437-446, December, 19

"Physicians' attitudes on the abortion law. Report of survey, 1969,' by R. G. Smith, et al. HAWAII MED J 29:209-211, January-February, 1970.

"Propos on abortion: apropos of a recent book," by J. E. Marcel. GYNEC PRAT 21:235-242, 1970.

"Reforming the abortion laws: a doctor looks at the case," by D. Cavanagh. AMERICA 122:406-411, April 18, 1970; Discussion 122:571, May 30, 1970.

"Registrar General's supplement on abortion," by P. Kestelman.

LANCET 2:566-567, September 12, 1970.

"Talk with two abortionists; interview," ed. by B. Buresh.
NEWSWEEK 75:61, April 13, 1970.

"You may be right. Therapeutic abortion in medical perspective,"
by J. E. Hodgson. MINN MED 53:755 passim, July, 1970.

POPULATION
"Abortion is the world's most common (and worst) population regulator," by G. Machanik. SA NURS J 36:32-33 passim, April, 1970.

"Abortion on request: Its consequences for population trends and
public health," by C. Tietze. SEMIN PSYCHIAT 2,3:375-381, 1970.

"Artificial pregnancy interruption and birth rate," by K. Vácha. CESK
GYNEK 35:329-330, July, 1970.

"Effect of induced abortion on birth rate: a simulation model," by S.
Mukherji, et al. INDIAN J PUBLIC HEALTH 14:49-58, January,
1970.

"Extended birth control: Abortion on request," by J. G. Howells. CAN
MENT HLTH 18:3+, September-October, 1970.

"Population crisis and extremism," by H. H. Suter. SCIENCE 168:
777, May 15, 1970.

"Study of cause of natural abortion: based on the data on natural abortion in 1967 socioeconomic population survey," by T. Suganuma,
et al. JAP J PUBLIC HEALTH NURSE 26:49-51, October, 1970.

"Study on the cause of natural abortion--based on the 1967 socio-
economic population survey," by T. Suganuma, et al. JAP J
MIDWIFE 24:50-56, October, 1970.

POST ABORTUM COMPLICATIONS
  see also: Complications
             Sepsis
             Septic Abortion & Septic Shock

POST ABORTUM COMPLICATIONS

"Abortion request and post-operative response. A Washington commu nity survey," by R. J. Pion, et al. NORTHWEST MED 69:693-698, September, 1970.

"2 cases of post abortum perfringens septicemia. Death," by P. L. Barraya, et al. BULL FED SOC GYNECOL OBSTET LANG FR 22:354-355, June-August, 1970.

"2 cases of post-abortum psychoses," by W. Pasini, et al. ANN MEDICOPSYCHOL 1:555-564, April, 1970.

"Certain indices of glucocorticold function of the adrenal cortex in postabortion sepsis," by M. G. Simakova. AKUSH GINEKOL 46: 14-18, February, 1970.

"Postabortal and postpartum tetanus," by B. K. Adadevoh, et al. J OBSTET GYNAECOL BR COMMONW 77:1019-1023, November 1970.

"Post-abortum hemorrhage caused by intravascula coagulation. Cure by hysterectomy," by J. Testart, et al. ANN CHIR 24:229-234, February, 1970.

"Prognosis and treatment of post-abortum acute renal insufficiency," by M. Legrain, et al. PRESSE MED 78:1565-1570, August 29, 19

"Rhesus sensitization following abortion," by H. Finger, et al. DEUTSCH MED WSCHR 95:1025-1028, May 1, 1970.

"Rh immunisation and abortion," LANCET 2:141, July 18, 1970.

"The threat of Rh immunisation from abortion," by V. J. Freda, et a LANCET 2:147-148, July 18, 1970.

"Use of a combination of an antibiotic with proteolytic enzymes in post-abortion pelvic infection," by E. Acosta Bendek. GINEC OBSTET MEX 27:297-305, March, 1970.

POTASSIUM PERMANGANATE
"Attempt at abortion with potassium permanganate tablets," by A. L Coz, et al. BULL FED SOC GYNECOL OBSTET LANG FR

20:190-191, April-May, 1968.

*REGNANCY INTERRUPTION
see: Induced Abortion

*REVENTION & CONTROL
see: Drug Therapy
Laws & Legislation

*ROGESTERONE
"Assessment of the obstetric application of 17-hydroxyprogesterone
caproate (Hormofort), " by S. Németi, et al. ORV HETIL 111:1404-
1407, June 14, 1970.

"Contractibility of the human uterus and the hormonal situation. Studies on therapy with progesterone in pregnancy," by P. Mentasti, et
al. MINERVA GINECOL 21:685-687, May 31, 1969.

"High doses of progesterone in the therapy of hormonal abortion and in
the prevention of various types of pregnancy interruption," by C.
Morra, et al. MINERVA GINECOL 21:699-701, May 31, 1969.

"Plasma progesterone levels during bougie-induced abortion in mid-
pregnancy," by Y. Manabe. J ENDOCR 46:127-128, January, 1970.

"Plasma progesterone levels during saline-induced abortion," by W. G.
Wiest, et al. J CLIN ENDOCR 30:774-777, June, 1970.

"Progestogen therapy in early pregnancy and associated congential
defects," by S. Dillon. PRACTITIONER 205:80-84, July, 1970.

"The relationship between progesterone, uterine volume, intrauterine
pressure, and clinical progress in hypertonic saline--induced
abortions," by A. I. Csapo, et al. AM J OBSTET GYNECOL 108:
950-955, November 15, 1970.

"Treatment of abortion with progesterone and etiology of abortion," by
M. Sakurabayashi. J JAP OBSTET GYNEC SOC 22:69-72, January,
1970.

"Treatment of threatened abortion with high doses of progesterone,"

PROGESTERONE

by P. Spanio, et al. MINERVA GINECOL 21:681-682, May 31, 19

"Therapy of threatened abortion with progestational hormones," by (
D. Montanari, et al. MINERVA GINECOL 21:683-684, May 31,
1969.

PROSTAGLANDINS

"Abortion without surgery? using prostaglandin F2 alpha," TIME 9!
39-40, February 9, 1970.

"Absence of antidiuresis during administration of prostaglandin F2
alpha," by G. Roberts, et al. BRIT MED J 2:152-154, April 18,
1970.

"Clinical use of prostaglandins," BR MED J 4:253-254, October 31
1970.

"Effect of prostaglandins on human uterus in pregnancy," by M. P.
Embrey. J REPROD FERTIL 23:372-373, November, 1970.

"Induction of abortion by prostaglandins E1 and E2," by M. P.
Embrey. BRIT MED J 1:258-260, May 2, 1970.

"Induction of therapeutic abortion with intravenous prostaglandin F,
by N. Wiqvist, et al. LANCET 1:889, April 25, 1970.

"Prostaglandins and the induction of labour or abortion," LANCET
1:927-928, May 2, 1970.

"Prostaglandins and spontaneous abortion," by S. M. Karim, et al
J OBSTET GYNAEC BRIT COMM 77:837-839, September, 1970.

"Prostaglandins for induction of therapeutic abortion," by U. Roth-
Brandel, et al. LANCET 1:190-191, January 24, 1970.

"Prostaglandins in fertility control," by S. M. Karim. LANCET 1:1'
May 23, 1970.

"Therapeutic abortion by local administration of prostaglandin," by
Wiqvist, et al. LANCET 2:716-717, October 3, 1970.

"Therapeutic abortion using prostaglandin F2 alpha," by S. M. Karim, et al. LANCET 1:157-159, January 24, 1970.

"Therapeutic abortions using prostaglandin E2," by G. M. Filshie. J REPROD FERTIL 23:371-372, November, 1970.

"Use of prostaglandin E2 in the management of missed abortion, missed labour, and hydatidiform mole," by S. M. Karim BRIT MED J 1:196-197, July 25. 1970.

"Use of prostaglandin E2 for therapeutic abortion," by S. M. Karim, et al. BRIT MED J 1:198-200, July 25, 1970.

PSYCHIATRY

"2 Cases of post-abortum psychoses," by W. Pasini, et al. ANN MEDICOPSYCHOL 1:555-564, April, 1970.

"Evaluation of therapeutic abortion as an element of preventive psychiatry," by H. G. Whittington. AMER J PSYCHIAT 126: 1224-1229, March, 1970.

"Law, preventive psychiatry, and therapeutic abortion," by H. I. Levene, et al. J NERV MENT DIS 151:51-59, July, 1970.

"Mental and sexual problems related to pregnancy interruption," by O. Kolářová. CESK GYNEK 35:378-379, July, 1970.

"Psychiatric experience with a liberalized therapeutic abortion law," by L. Marder. AMER J PSYCHIAT 126:1230-1236, March, 1970.

"Psychiatric indications for the termination of pregnancy," MED J AUST 2:12 12-1213, December 19, 1970.

"Psychiatric indications for therapeutic abortion," by C. W. Butler. SOUTHERN MED J 63:647-650, June, 1970.

"Psychiatric indications or psychiatric justification of therapeutic abortion?" by E. Pfeiffer. ARCH GEN PSYCHIATRY 23:402-407, November, 1970.

"Psychologic and emotional consequences of elective abortion. A review," by G. S. Walter. OBSTET GYNEC 36:482-491, Septemb 1970 (161 ref.).

"Psychological and emotional indications for therapeutic abortion," N. M. Simon. SEMIN PSYCHIAT 2,3:283-301, 1970.

"Some psychiatric aspects of abortion," by S. Fleck. J NERV MEN' DIS 151:42-50, July, 1970 (42 ref.).

"Termination of pregnancy on psychiatric grounds," by J. Johnson. MANCH MED GAZ 49:10, July, 1970.

RELIGION
see: Sociology

RHOGAM
"RhoGam--current status," by K. P. Russell. CALIF MED 113:44-4 December, 1970.

"The role of RhoGam in therapeutic and spontaneous abortion," by Sprague. HAWAII MED J 29:450-451, July-August, 1970.

SEPSIS
"2 cases of post abortum perfringens septicemia. Death," by P. L. Barraya, et al. BULL FED SOC GYNECOL OBSTET LANG FR 354-355, June-August, 1970.

"Certain indices of glucocorticold function of the adrenal cortex in postabortion sepsis," by M. G. Simakova. AKUSH GINEKOL 46 18, February, 1970.

"Clinical and x-ray aspects of pulmonary edema in patients with se following abortion," by Kh. A. Khidirbeil, et al. VESTN RENTG RADIOL 45:77-82, March-April, 1970.

"Maternal deaths due to sepsis with septic shock," OHIO MED J 66:589-591, June, 1970.

"Pathogenesis, clinical aspects and therapy of inflammatory diseas AKUSH GINEK 46:21-31, April, 1970.

"Pregnancy and labor in patients with interventricular and inter-arterial septal defects," by A. L. Beĭlin. AKUSH GINEKOL 46: 16-19, May, 1970.

"Staphylococcal septicemia. Comments on a case of staphyolococcal septicemia," by I. Zorlescu. MUNCA SANIT 18:682-685, November, 1970.

"The use of hyperbaric oxygen in the treatment of clostridial septicemia complicating septic abortion. Report of a case," by L. E. Perrin, et al. AMER J OBSTET GYNEC 106:666-668, March, 1970.

EPTIC ABORTION
see: Septic Abortion & Septic Shock

EPTIC ABORTION & SEPTIC SHOCK
see also: Post Abortum Complications
Septic Abortion
Sepsis

"Agressive management of incomplete or inevitable abortion. Report of 1002 septic and aseptic patients," by J. L. Breen, et al. J MED SOC NJ 67:711-715, November, 1970.

"Bacteremia shock syndrome in obstetrics," by I. Szemesi, et al. ACTA CHIR ACAD SCI HUNG 11:87-95, 1970.

"A case of bacteremic shock with acute pulmonary edema during abortion," by F. Charvet, et al. BULL FED GYNEC OBSTET FRANC 22:67, January-March, 1970.

"Cephaloridine in septic abortion. Comparison with a conventional combined antibiotic regimen in a conservative program of management," by W. E. Josey, et al. AMER J OBSTET GYNEC 106:237-242, January 15, 1970.

"Clostridial organisms in septic abortions. Report of 7 cases," by R. T. O'Neill, et al. OBSTET GYNEC 35:458-461, March, 1970.

"Comparison of two antibiotic regimens in the treatment of septic abortion," by D. R. Ostergard. OBSTET GYNEC 36:473-474, September, 1970.

"Maternal deaths due to sepsis with septic shock," OHIO MED J 66 589-591, June, 1970.

"Medical grand rounds at Yale-New Haven Hospital. Septic abortion," F. L. Sachs, et al. CONN MED 34:649-653, September, 1970.

"Oral administration of an association of an antibiotic, enzymes and balsam in septic inflammatory diseases in gynecology and obstet rics," by G. Locardi. MINERVA MED 61:961-965, March 10, 197

"Practical management of septic abortion," by J. C. Caillouette, et HOSP MED 6:29+, January, 1970.

"Septic abortion and septic shock," by B. A. Santamarina, et al. CL OBSTET GYNECOL 13:291-304, June, 1970 (24 ref.).

"Septic abortion--current management," by J. C. Caillouette. CALIF MED 113:44, December, 1970.

"Septic abortion with endotoxic shock," by D. Cavanagh, et al. AUS NZ J OBSTET GYNAECOL 10:160-166, August, 1970.

"Septic incomplete abortion. A retrospective study of twenty years' perience," by D. R. Ostergard, et al. OBSTET GYNEC 35:709-7 May, 1970.

"Septic shock," by L. Heller, et al. ZBL GYNAEK 92:111-119, Jan ary 24, 1970.

"Septic threatened abortion. A retrospective study of twenty years' perience," by J. G. Bradley, et al. OBSTET GYNEC 35:714-717 May, 1970.

"Treatment of septic abortion and septic shock," by B. A. Santamar et al. MOD TREAT 7:779-788, July, 1970.

"Visual function in septic abortion," by E. I. Khvat. VESTN OFTA MOL 5:89-90, 1970.

SEXUAL DISORDERS
  see: Complications
       Induced Abortion

SOCIOLOGY
  see *also*: Family Planning

"Abortion analysis," by P. Diggory. LANCET 2:413-414, August 22, 1970.

"Abortion and the just society," by N. F. Isaacs. RJT 5:27, 1970.

"Abortion and sterilization. Status of the law in mid-1970," by N. Hershey. AMER J NURS 70:1926-1927, September, 1970.

"Abortion and suicidal behaviors: observations on the concept of endangering the mental health of the mother," by H. L. P. Resnik, et al. MENTAL HYGIENE 55:10-20, January, 1970.

"Abortion attitudes of poverty level blacks," by C. E. Vincent, et al. SEMIN PSYCHIAT 2,3:309-317, 1970.

"Abortion capital," by C. B. Goodhart. LANCET 1:367, February 14, 1970.

"Abortion caravan," by K. Maeots. CAN FORUM 50:157, July-August, 1970.

"Abortion: The Catholic viewpoint," by F. J. Ayd, Jr. SEMIN PSYCHIAT 2,3:258-262, 1970.

"Abortion: change of heart," NATURE 227:11, July 4, 1970.

"Abortion comes out of the shadows," LIFE 68:20B, February 27, 1970.

"Abortion: crime or privilege?" by J. M. Hannaford. MAYO CLIN PROC 45:510-516, July, 1970.

"Abortion dogmas needing research scrutiny," by E. Pohlman. SEMIN PSYCHIAT 2,3:220-230, 1970.

"Abortion incorporated," JAMA 214:362, October 12, 1970.

"Abortion is no man's business," by N. Shainess. PSYCHOLOGY TC 3:18-24, May, 1970.

"Abortion: law, ethics and the value of life," by C. Burke. MANCH N GAZ 49:4-9, July, 1970.

"Abortion laws: a study in social change," by T. G. Moyers. SAN DI L REV 7:237, May, 1970.

"Abortion: the lonely problem," RN 33:34-39, June, 1970.

"Abortion: The medical and psychological view," by J. E. Brody WOMAN'S DAY 34:68+, October, 1970.

"Abortion: new studies," COMMONWEAL 93:76-77, October 16, 1970

"Abortion on request: Its consequences for population trends and put health," by C. Tietze. SEMIN PSYCHIAT 2,3:375-381, 1970.

"Abortion or no? What decides? An inquiry by questionnaire into the attitudes of gynecologists and psychiatrists in Aberdeen," by C. McCance, et al. SEMIN PSYCHIAT 2,3:352-360, 1970.

"Abortion--a stormy subject," RN 33:53+, September, 1970.

"The abortion survey," by J. L. Moore, Jr. J MED ASSOC GA 59:45 460, December, 1970.

"Abortion: a theologian's view," by P. R. Ramsey. AORN J 12:55-6 November, 1970.

"Abortion tumult," SR SCHOL 96:7-8, May 4, 1970.

"Abortion unlimited," NEWSWEEK 75:46, March 9, 1970.

"Abortion--where do we go from here?" by D. Cashman. CATH NURS 32:22-27, March, 1970.

"Abortion: yes or no?" by R. B. Zachary. MANCH MED GAZ 50:4-5 October, 1970.

"Anti-abortion lobby; Catholic resistance to New York state's bill,"
by J. Deedy. COMMONWEAL 92:154, May 1, 1970; Discussion 92:
255, May 22, 1970.

"Background of a lost baby," by B. J. Hughes. NURS MIRROR 131:
46-48, October 23, 1970.

"A case against abortion: plea for the unborn child," by M. A. Duffy.
NEW YORK LAW JOURNAL 164:1+, September 23, 1970.

"Catholics and abortion," by W. F. Buckley, Jr. NAT R 2:1366-1367,
December 15, 1970.

"Cause of action for "wrongful life": a suggested analysis," MINN L
REV 55:58, November, 1970.

"Christian choices in a liberal abortion climate," by R. F. R. Gardner.
CHR TODAY 14:6-8, May 22, 1970.

"Civil status and risks of abortion, premature childbirth and perinatal
death," by F. Pettersson. LAKARTIDNINGEN 67:3369-3372,
July 22, 1970.

"Consent to continued pregnancy," by R. Matz. N ENGL J MED 283:
1522-1523, December 31, 1970.

"The culture of poverty in relation to disease in Latin America," by L.
S. Miranda. P RICO ENFERM 45:14-15 concl, March, 1970.

"The Declaration of Oslo," S AFR MED J 44:1281, November 14, 1970.

"Earth Day revisited," by A. Savage. IMPRINT 17:8, September-
October, 1970.

"The ethics of abortion," by C. W. Sem-Jacobsen, et al. AMER J
PSYCHIAT 127:536-538, October, 1970.

"Feticide infanticide upon request," by P. Ramsey. RELIGION IN LIFE
39:170-186, Summer, 1970.

"Free abortion," by L. Valvanne. KATILOLEHTI 75:91, March, 1970.

101

"Happier birthdays; the story of the National Birthday Trust," by J. Barnes. MIDWIVES CHRON 83:406-411, December, 1970.

"How men feel about abortion," by C. Karpel. MLLE 71:142-143 , June, 1970.

"Human rights - What of the unborn," NEW ZEALAND NURS J 63:4 July, 1970.

"I'm married, happy, and went through hell for a legal abortion," by Squire. PORT MACL MAG 83:51-52, 54-56, October, 1970.

"Improving the quality of life," by C. E. Flowers, Jr. ALA J MED S 7:297-299, July, 1970.

"Is abortion a right? symposium," CHR CENT 87:624-631, May 20, 1970; Discussion 87:972-973, August 12, 1970.

"Isolating the male bias against reform of abortion legislation," SAl CLARA LAW 10:301, Spring, 1970.

"Legal abortion and social class," by W. H. James. LANCET 2:65! September 26, 1970.

"Looking back at Luenbach: 296 non-hospital abortions. (Luenbach by E. B. Keemer, Jr. J NAT MED ASS 62:291-293, July, 1970.

"Male use of contraception and attitudes toward abortion, Santiago, Chile, 1968 (responses in a survey)," by M. Francoise Hall. MIl BANK MEMORIAL FUND Q 48:145-166, April, 1970.

" "The massacre of the innocents: apropos of a proposed law to legal abortions under many circumstances," by E. Aubertin. BORDEA MED 3:1873-1882, July-August, 1970.

"Mental and sexual problems related to pregnancy interruption," by Kolářová. CESK GYNEK 35:378-379, July, 1970.

"The moral muddle," CATH NURSE 32:4-5, June, 1970.

"Morality of abortion; views," by D. Callahan, et al. NEWSWEEK 75:64-65, June 8, 1970.

"My thoughts about abortion and premature births," by N. Tsutsumi. KANGO 22:184-186, March, 1970.

"Not fit to print? New York bishops' pastoral letter," by S. J. Adamo. AMERICA 123:568-570, December 26, 1970.

"Number one method," NATION 210:69-70, January 26, 1970.

"Psychological aspects of abortion in Czechoslovakia," by Z. Dytrych. J PSYCHIAT NURS 8:30-33, May-June, 1970.

"Psychological aspects of habitual abortion," by M. Silverman, et al. PSYCHIATR COMMUN 13:35-43, 1970.

"Only her doctor knows," CHR TODAY 14:35-36, April 24, 1970.

"Open letter to American doctors," AMERICA 122:490-491, May 9, 1970.

"The origin of human life," T ZIEKENVERP 23:32-36, January 6, 1970.

"Papal fallibility," CHR CENT 87:1309, November 4, 1970; Discussion 88:21, January 6, 1970.

"Perverse observations on abortion," by P. J. Weber. CATH WORLD 212:74-77, November, 1970.

"The preservation of life," by N. K. Brown, et al. JAMA 211:76-82, January 5, 1970.

"Psychosocial aspects of therapeutic abortion," by L. Marder, et al. SOUTHERN MED J 63:657-661, June, 1970.

"Psychosocial studies in family planning behavior in Central and Eastern Europe. A preliminary report of a developing program," by H. P. David. J PSYCHIATR NURS 8:28-33, September-October, 1970.

"Reasons for abortion," BRIT MED J 3:362, August 15, 1970.

"Reasons for abortion," by D. G. Clyne. BR MED J 3:769-770, September 26, 1970.

"Recommended standards for abortion services. Adopted by the Exe tive Board of the APHA at the 98th Annual Meeting in Houston, Texas, October 29, 1970.

"Religious aspects and theology in therapeutic abortion," by J. E. Herndon. SOUTHERN MED J 63:651-654, June, 1970.

"Right to live," by J. R. Quinn. AMERICA 123:56-57, August 8, 1970

"The right to live," by J. Stallworthy. J ROY COLL GEN PRACT 187-190, April, 1970.

"Right to privacy: does it allow a woman the right to determine whe to bear children?" AM U L REV 20:136, August, 1970.

"The role of human conscience in therapeutic abortion," by P. R. Sullivan. AM J PSYCHIATRY 127:250, August, 1970.

"Searching of truth on abortion," by E. Hervet. GYNEC OBSTET 6 287-295, May-July, 1970.

"Similarly I will not--cause abortion," by R. D. Knapp, Jr. J LA ST MED SOC 122:297-301, October, 1970.

"Social workers and abortion," by E. F. Ford. WOM R REVOLUTIO LIBERATION 1,2:18-19, Winter, 1970.

"State of the abortion question," by R. F. Drinan. COMMONWEAL 108-109, April 17, 1970; Reply with rejoinder. by E. MacNeil 9. 283+, June 12, 1970.

"Study on the cause of natural abortion--based on the 1967 socio-ec ic population survey," by T. Suganuma, et al. JAP J MIDWIFE 50-56, October, 1970.

"Survey on eugenics with special reference to public awareness," b Matsuura, et al. J JAP MED ASS 63:1516-1520, June 15, 1970.

"Troubled waters," by M. T. Southgate. JAMA 213:1182-1183, August 17, 1970.

"The truth about abortion in New York," by R. E. Hall. COLUMBIA FORUM 13:18-22, Winter, 1970.

"Victims: interviews," RAMP MAG 9:23-25, August, 1970.

"Voluntary abortion," by R. Mahon. BULL INFIRM CATHOL CAN 37: 219-225, September-December, 1970.

"War on the womb," CHR TODAY 14:24-25, June 5, 1970.

"What men should be told about abortion," by N. V. Don. FELDSH AKUSH 35:45-46, June, 1970.

SPONTANEOUS ABORTION

"Aberrant karyotypes and spontaneous abortion in a Japanses family," by T. Kadotani, et al. NATURE 225:735-737, February 21, 1970.

"Aging of fertilizing gametes and spontaneous abortion. Effect of the day of ovulation and the time of insemination," by R. Guerrero, et al. AMER J OBSTET GYNEC 107:263-267, May 15, 1970.

"Anatomic and chromosomal anomalies in spontaneous abortion. Possible correlation with overripeness of oocytes," by K. Mikamo. AMER J OBSTET GYNEC 106:243-254, January 15, 1970.

"Association of maternal genital herpetic infection with spontaneous abortion," by Z. M. Naib, et al. OBSTET GYNEC 35:260-263, February, 1970.

"Attempts to isolate H-1 virus from spontaneous human abortions: a negative report," by S. J. Newman, et al. TERATOLOGY 3:279-281, August, 1970.

"Chromosomal abnormalities and spontaneous abortion," MED J AUST 2:992-994, November 28, 1970.

"Chromosomal anomalies in spontaneously aborted human fetuses," by R. K. Dhadial, et al. LANCET 2:20-21, July 4, 1970.

"Chromosome abberations in human spontaneous abortion," by J. G Boué, et al. PRESSE MED 78:635-641, May 21, 1970.

"Chromosome aberrations in spontaneous abortion," by P. Dráč, et CESK GYNEK 35:230-233, May, 1970 (42 ref.).

"Chromosome studies in selected spontaneous abortions. 1. Concep after oral contraceptives," by D. H. Carr. CANAD MED ASS J 343-348, August 15, 1970.

"Chromosomes in spontaneous abortions," by B. Padeh, et al. HAR FUAH 78:158-161, February 15, 1970.

"Cytogenetics of spontaneous abortion. The chromosomes of decidu by D. T. Arakaki, et al. AMER J OBSTET GYNEC 107:1199-12 August 15, 1970.

"Fetal erythrocytes in maternal circulation after spontaneous aborti by O. Litwak, et al. JAMA 214:531-534, October 19, 1970.

"Immunoglobulins in spontaneous abortion and ectopic pregnancy," R. T. O'Neill, et al. OBSTET GYNEC 36:264-267, August, 197

"Infection of the fetus by Candida in a spontaneous abortion," by C Ho, et al. AMER J OBSTET GYNEC 106:705-710, March, 1970.

"Placenta and chromosome aberrations in spontaneous abortion," b Philippe, et al. PRESSE MED 78:641-646, March 21, 1970.

"Prostaglandins and spontaneous abortion," by S. M. Karim, et al. J OBSTET GYNAEC BRIT COMM 77:837-839, September, 1970.

"The role of RhoGam in therapeutic and spontaneous abortion," by Sprague. HAWAII MED J 29:450-451, July-August, 1970.

"Spontaneous abortion and human pesticide residues of DDT and D' by J. A. O'Leary, et al. AM J OBSTET GYNECOL 108:1291-12 December 15, 1970.

"Spontaneous and induced abortion. Report of a WHO scientific gro

WHO TECH REP SER 461:3-51, 1970.

"Transplacental hemorrhage during spontaneous and therapeutic artificial abortion," by J. A. Goldman, et al. OBSTET GYNEC 35:903-908, June, 1970.

STATISTICS

"Abortion goes public. Hospitals report 2,000 abortions in first week under new N. Y. law," MOD HOSP 115:33-36, August, 1970.

"The abortion survey," by J. L. Moore, Jr. J MED ASSOC GA 59: 459-460, December, 1970.

"1,229 cases of abortion in the Caldas University Hospital," by O. Vélez Ramirez. REV COLOMBIA OBSTET GINEC 21:147-170, March-April, 1970.

"Sex ratio in human embryos obtained from induced abortion: histological examination of the gonad in 1,452 cases," by S. Lee, et al. AM J OBSTET GYNECOL 108:1294-1297, December 15, 1970.

STERILITY

"Control of fertility," by M. L. Peterson. NEW ENG J MED 282: 1432-1433, June 18, 1970.

Fertility control: health and educational factors for the 1970s. Contraception or abortion?" by J. H. Hughes. J BIOSOC SCI 2:161-166, April, 1970.

"Ideal means of fertility control?" by A. Gillespie, et al. LANCET 1: 717, April 4, 1970.

"Long-term follow up of secondary sterility following artificial interruption of pregnancy," by O. Kolářová. CESK GYNEKOL 35:399-400, September, 1970.

"Prostaglandins in fertility control," by S. M. Karim. LANCET 1:1115, May 23, 1970.

"Signigicance of sterility following artificial interruption of pregnancy," by M. Kohoutek, et al. CESK GYNEKOL 35:398-399,

STERILITY

September, 1970.

"Sterility following artificial interruption of 1st pregnancy," by K. Jirátko, et al. CESK GYNEKOL 35:397-398, September, 1970.

STERILITY OR STERILIZATION
"Abortion and sterilization. Status of the law in mid-1970," by N. Hershey. AMER J NURS 70:1926-1927, September, 1970.

"Aging of fertilizing gametes and spontaneous abortion. Effect of the day of ovulation and the time of insemination," by R. Guerrero, e al. AMER J OBSTET GYNEC 107:263-267, May 15, 1970.

"College policy on abortion and sterilization," ACOG NURSES BUL 4:2, Fall, 1970.

"Surgical nursing: Abortions and sterilizations," REGAN REP NUR! LAW 11:1, June, 1970.

STUDENTS
"Abortion: the academic angle," MLLE 72:145, December, 1970.

"College policy on abortion and sterilization," ACOG NURSES BUL 4:2, Fall, 1970.

"College students' attitudes toward abortion," by J. W. Maxwell. FA COORDINATOR 19,3:247-252, July, 1970.

SURGICAL TREATMENT & MANAGEMENT
"Agressive management of incomplete or inevitable abortion. Report of 1002 septic and aseptic patients," by J. L. Breen, et al. J MED SOC NJ 67:711-715, November, 1970.

"Effective surgical procedures for interruption of pregnancy in the second trimester," by Y. Onishi. SANFUJIN JISSAI 19:73-78, January, 1970.

"Failures of cervix uteri cerclage due to a fault of technic," by M. Dumont, et al. BULL FED SOC GYNECOL OBSTET LANG FR 22:473, September-October, 1970.

"Habitual abortion and premature labor caused by primary cervical insufficiency. Surgical and pharmacological treatment," by G. Colucci, et al. MINERVA GINECOL 21:687-688, May 31, 1969.

"How to perform abortion in the 2d trimester," by J. Presl CESK GYNEKOL 35:437-438, September, 1970.

"Interruption of late term pregnancy by means of vaginal cesarean section," by Z. Ia. Gendon. AKUSH GINEK 46:58-61, January, 1970.

"Isthmus insufficiency treated by cerclage operation," by K. Bang. UGESKR LAEG 132:734-736, April 16, 1970.

"The management of missed abortion," by G. J. Ratten. AUST NZ J OBSTET GYNAECOL 10:115-118, May, 1970.

"Peritoneal puncture in emergency traumatology," SIONS 15:357-358 passim, September-October, 1970.

"Primary indication of surgical pregnancy interruption," by M. Chalupa, et al. CESK GYNEK 35:344-345, July, 1970.

"A scheme in the management of threatened abortion," by V. Ruiz Velasco, et al. GINEC OBSTET MEX 28:209-218, August, 1970.

"Scientific organization of the work of medical personnel in surgery for the interruption of early pregnancy," by A. A. Bagrov, et al. AKUSH GINEKOL 46:69-70, November, 1970.

"Successful surgical management of uterine anomalies in habitual abortions," by A. Zwinger, et al. CESK GYNEK 35:275-277, 1970.

"Surgery of isthmico-cervical insufficiency during pregnancy using the modified Szendi method," by M. A. Niiazova. AKUSH GINEK 46: 35-38, January, 1970.

"Surgical nursing: Abortions and sterilizations," REGAN REP NURS LAW 11:1, June, 1970.

"Surgical treatment of cervical incompetence during pregnancy," by D. Kaskarelis, et al. INT SURG 53:296-299, April, 1970.

"Surgical treatment of uterine cervix incompetence by means of circu suture concomitant with the suturing of the lateral edges of the ex ternal orifice of the cervix uteri," by R. Wawryk, et al. GINEKOL POL 41:985-988, September, 1970.

"Vacuum curettage. Out patient curettage without anesthesia. A repo of 350 cases," by J. G. Jensen. DAN MED BULL 17,7:199-209, 1970.

TECHNIQUES OF ABORTION

"Combined use of the aspiration method and abortion forceps in induc abortion between the 13th and 18th week of pregnancy," by A. Atanasov, et al. AKUSH GINEKOL (Sofiia) 9:223-228, 1970.

"Come and go" aspiration abortion," by A. J. Margolis. CALIF MED 113:43, December, 1970.

"Complications in the interruption of abortion, depending on the meth used--classical or aspiration method," by A. Atanasov. AKUSK GINEKOL (Sofiia) 9:271-277, 1970.

"Critical study of mono-and diphasic methods of artificial interruptio of pregnancy," by W. Weise, et al. ZBL GYNAK 92,26:841-848, 1970.

"Fracture of curette," by J. M. McGarry. BRIT MED J 1:49, January 3, 1970.

"Intrauterine curettage and the capacity of blood coagulation," by N. Shinagawa, et al. SANFUJIN JISSAI 19:758-762, July, 1970.

"Pregnancy interruption by means of vibrodilation and vacuum aspir- ation," by J. Német, et al. ZBL GYNAEK 92:120-127, January 2 1970.

"Scientific organization of the work of medical personnel in surgery for the interruption of early pregnancy," by A. A. Bagrov, et al.

TECHNIQUES OF ABORTION

AKUSH GINEKOL 46:69-70, November, 1970.

"The suction curette in termination of pregnancy," by D. Pfanner, et al. MED J AUST 2:733, October 17, 1970.

"Techniques of abortion," by W. J. Cameron. J KANS MED SOC 71: 375-377, October, 1970.

"Termination hysterectomy," by A. C. Lewis, et al. J OBSTET GYNAEC BRIT COMM 77:743-744, August, 1970.

"The use of suction curettage in incomplete abortion," by P. E. Suter, et al. J OBSTET GYNAEC BRIT COMM 77:464-466, May, 1970.

"Vacuum aspiration in therapeutic abortion," by B. Barmen. T NORSK LAEGEFOREN 90:15-16, January 1, 1970.

"Vacuum aspiration for the therapeutic abortion," by H. Jenssen. T NORSK LAEGEFOREN 90:19-21, 'anuary 1, 1970.

"Vacuum aspiration in therapeutic and incomplete abortion," by J. C. Aure. T NORSK LAEGEFOREN 90:16-18, January 1, 1970.

"Vacuum aspiration of the uterus in therapeutic abortion," by A. E. Buckle, et al. BRIT MED J 1:456-457, May 23, 1970.

"Vacuum curettage. Out patient curettage without anasthesia. A report of 350 cases," by J. G. Jensen. DAN MED BULL 17,7:199-209, 1970.

TERMINATION
see: Therapeutic Abbortion

THERAPEUTIC ABORTION
"Cytohormonal studies of vaginal smears performed during the treatment of imminent abortions," by B. Wierstakow, et al. GINEKOL POL 41:977-984, September, 1970.

"The effect of oxytocin on the complication rate of early therapeutic abortions," by E. D. B. Johansson. ACTA OBSTET GYNEC SCAND 49,2:129-131, 1970.

"The effects of anesthesia and pulmonary ventilation on blood loss during elective therapeutic abortion," by B. F. Cullen, et al. ANESTHESIOLOGY 32:108-113, February, 1970.

"Effects of anesthesia in therapeutic abortion," by W. H. Forrest, Jr. ANESTHESIOLOGY 33:121-122, July, 1970.

"Evaluation of therapeutic abortion as an element of preventive psychiatry," by H. G. Whittington. AMER J PSYCHIAT 126:1224-1229, March, 1970.

"Experience at Duke Medical Center after modern legislation for therapeutic abortion," by A. C. Christakos. SOUTHERN MED J 63:655-657, June, 1970.

"Fetal indications for termination of pregnancy," by H. L. Nadler. SEMIN PSYCHIAT 2,3:302-308, 1970.

"Feto-maternal haemorrhage at therapeutic abortion," by A. H. John, et al. J OBSTET GYNAEC BRIT COMM 77:137-138, February, 1970.

"Follow-up of patients referred for termination of pregnancy," by C. M Pare, et al. LANCET 1:635-638, March 28, 1970.

"General practitioners' views on pregnancy termination," by W. Sussman, et al. MED J AUST 2:169-173, July 25, 1970.

"The gynecologist and therapeutic abortion: the changing times," by P. R. DeAluarez, et al. SEMIN PSYCHIAT 2,3:275-282, 1970.

"The immediate morbidity of therapeutic abortion," by M. A. Carlton, et al. MED J AUST 2:1071-1074, December 5, 1970.

"Importance of the fundamentals: practical key points in practice of therapeutic abortion," by M. Iwata. SANFUJIN JISSAI 19:339-345, April, 1970.

"Induction of therapeutic abortion with intravenous prostaglandin F," by N. Wiqvist, et al. LANCET 1:889, April 25, 1970.

"Is therapeutic abortion preventable?" by W. Droegemueller, et al. OBSTET GYNEC 35:758-759, May, 1970.

"Law, preventive psychiatry, and therapeutic abortion," by H. I. Levene, et al. J NERV MENT DIS 151:51-59, July, 1970.

"Kovacs' semiconservative method of pregnancy interruption," by I. Vido, et al. CESK GYNEK 35:345-347, July, 1970.

"Premature termination of pregnancy following previous artificial interruption of pregnancy," by P. Dráč, et al. CESK GYNEK 35:332-333, July, 1970.

"Prostaglandins for induction of therapeutic abortion," by U. Roth-Brandel, et al. LANCET 1:190-191, January 24, 1970.

"Psychiatric experience with a liberalized therapeutic abortion law," by L. Marder. AMER J PSYCHIAT 126:1230-1236, March, 1970.

"Psychiatric indications or psychiatric justification of therapeutic abortion?" by E. Pfeiffer. ARCH GEN PSYCHIATRY 23:402-407, November, 1970.

"Psychiatric indications for the termination of pregnancy," MED J AUST 2:1212-1213, December 19, 1970.

"Psychiatric indications for therapeutic abortion," by C. W. Butler. SOUTHERN MED J 63:647-650, June, 1970.

"Psychological and emotional indications for therapeutic abortion," by N. M. Simon. SEMIN PSYCHIAT 2,3:283-301, 1970.

"Psychosocial aspects of therapeutic abortion," by L. Marder, et al. SOUTHERN MED J 63:657-661, June, 1970.

"Religious aspects and theology in therapeutic abortion," by J. E. Herndon. SOUTHERN MED J 63:651-654, June, 1970.

"Right not to be born: refusal to grant therapeutic abortion in case of rubella baby," by M. K. Sanders. HARPER 240:92-99, April, 1970

"The role of fetal death in the process of therapeutic abortion induced by intra-amniotic injection of hypertonic saline," by L. Kovács, et al. J OBSTET GYNAECOL BR COMMONW 77:1132-1136, December, 1970.

"The role of human conscience in therapeutic abortion," by P. R. Sullivan. AM J PSYCHIATRY 127:250, August, 1970.

"The role of RhoGam in therapeutic and spontaneous abortion," by C. Sprague. HAWAII MED J 29:450-451, July-August, 1970.

"Saline versus glucose as a hypertonic solution for abortion," by W. Droegemueller, et al. AM J OBSTET GYNECOL 108:606-609, October 15, 1970.

"Some observations regarding unwanted pregnancies and therapeutic abortions," by C. P. Kimball. OBSTET GYNEC 35:293-296, February, 1970.

"The suction curette in termination of pregnancy," by D. Pfanner, et al. MED J AUST 2:733, October 17, 1970.

"Survey of therapeutic abortion committees," by K. D. Smith, et al. CRIM L Q 12:279, July, 1970.

"Termination hysterectomy," by A. C. Lewis, et al. J OBSTET GYNAEC BRIT COMM 77:743-744, August, 1970.

"Termination of pregnancy," by D. M. Potts. BRIT MED BULL 26: 65-71, January, 1970 (60 ref.).

"Termination of pregnancy on psychiatric grounds," by J. Johnson. MANCH MED GAZ 49:10, July, 1970.

"Therapeutic abortion," CALIF NURSE 66:1, December, 1970.

"Therapeutic abortion," by P. G. Coffey. CAN MED ASSOC J 103: 1194 passim, November 21, 1970.

THERAPEUTIC ABORTION

"Therapeutic abortion," by C. P. Harrison. CANAD MED ASS J 102: 1209-1211, May 30, 1970.

"Therapeutic abortion," by W. H. Pearse. NEBRASKA NURSE 3:6-7, May, 1970.

"Therapeutic abortion," by J. Stallworthy. PRACTITIONER 204:393-400, March, 1970.

"Therapeutic abortion. Clinical aspects," by E. C. Senay. ARCH GEN PSYCHIATRY 23:408-415, November, 1970.

"Therapeutic abortion. A two-year experience in one hospital," by H. Thompson, et al. JAMA 213:991-995, August 10, 1970.

"Therapeutic abortion. Washington, D.C.," by E. J. Connor, et al. MED ANN DC 39,3:133-137 & 186, 1970.

"Therapeutic abortion by local administration of prostaglandin," by N. Wiqvist, et al. LANCET 2:716-717, October 3, 1970.

"Therapeutic abortion in a Canadian city," by R. M. Boyce, et al. CAN MED ASSOC J 103:461-466, September 12, 1970.

"Therapeutic abortion in Great Britain," by D. A. Pond. SEMIN PSYCHIAT 2,3:336-340, 1970.

"Therapeutic abortion--the other side of the coin," by Z. M. Lebsensohn. MED ANN DC 39:275-277, May, 1970.

"Therapeutic abortion using prostaglandin F2 alpha," by S. M. Karim, et al. LANCET 1:157-159, January 24, 1970.

"Therapeutic abortion--Washington, D. C.," by E. J. Connor, et al. MED ANN DC 39:133-137 passim, March, 1970.

"Therapeutic abortion--who may have it?" by N. N. Chowdhury. J INDIAN MED ASS 54:163-164, February 16, 1970.

"Therapeutic abortions at University Hospitals, 1951-1969, with

115

emphasis on current trends," by D. W. Wetrich, et al. J IOWA MED SOC 60:691-696, October, 1970.

"Therapeutic abortions, 1963-1968," by C. Tietze. STUDIES IN FAMILY PLANNING 59:5-7, November, 1970.

"Therapeutic abortions using prostaglandin E2," by G. M. Filshie. J REPROD FERTIL 23:371-372, November, 1970.

"Transplacental haemorrhage due to termination of pregnancy," by J. J. Walsh, et al. J OBSTET GYNAEC BRIT COMM 77:133-136, February, 1970.

"Transplacental hemorrhage during spontaneous and therapeutic artificial abortion," by J. A. Goldman, et al. OBSTET GYNEC 35:903-908, June, 1970.

"Transplacental hemorrhage in patients subjected to therapeutic abortion," by T. H. Parmley, et al. AMER J OBSTET GYNEC 106: 540-542, February 15, 1970.

"Twin survival in therapeutic abortion," by C. P. Douglas. BR MED J 3:769, September 26, 1970.

"Unusual sequel to therapeutic abortion," by R. McDonald. LANCET 1:1118, May 23, 1970.

"Use of prostaglandin E2 for therapeutic abortion," by S. M. Karim, et al. BRIT MED J 1:198-200, July 25, 1970.

"Vacuum aspiration for the therapeutic abortion," by H. Jenssen. T NORSK LAEGEFOREN 90:19-21, January 1, 1970.

"Vacuum aspiration in therapeutic abortion," by B. Barmen. T NORSK LAEGEFOREN 90:15-16, January 1, 1970.

"Vacuum aspiration in therapeutic and incomplete abortion," by J. C. Aure. T NORSK LAEGEFOREN 90:16-18, January 1, 1970.

"Vacuum aspiration of the uterus in therapeutic abortion," by A. E. Buckle, et al. BRIT MED J 1:456-457, May 23, 1970.

THERAPEUTIC ABORTION

"Whither therapeutic abortion?" by D. Hay. MANCH MED GAZ 50:7-10 passim, October, 1970.

"The W.M.A. statement on therapeutic abortion," MED J AUST 2:484-485, September 12, 1970.

"You may be right. Therapeutic abortion in medical perspective," by J. E. Hodgson. MINN MED 53:755 passim, July, 1970.

TOXOPLASMAS

"Importance of toxoplasmosis in abortion," by P. Spanio. MINERVA GINECOL 21:693-694, May 31, 1969.

"Toxoplasmosis: abortions and stillbirths," by V. Hingorani, et al. INDIAN J MED RES 58:967-974, July, 1970.

"Toxoplasmosis and abortion. Serologic findings and clinical results," by M. Mega, et al. MINERVA GINECOL 21:694-695, May 31, 1969.

TRANSPLACENTAL HEMORRHAGE
see also: Hemorrhage

"Placental acetylcholine in induction of premature labor," by R. C. Goodlin. AMER J OBSTET GYNEC 107:429-431, June 1, 1970.

"Transplacental haemorrhage after abortion," by J. M. Bowman. LANCET 1:1108, May 23, 1970.

"Transplacental haemorrhage after abortion," by S. Murray, et al. LANCET 1:631-634, March 28, 1970.

"Transplacental haemorrhage after abortion," by G. Neubauer. LANCET 1:952, May 2, 1970.

"Transplacental haemorrhage due to termination of pregnancy," by J. J. Walsh, et al. J OBSTET GYNAEC BRIT COMM 77:133-136, February, 1970.

"Transplacental hemorrhage during spontaneous and therapeutic artificial abortion," by J. A. Goldman, et al. OBSTET GYNEC

TRANSPLACENTAL HEMORRHAGE

35:903-908, June, 1970.

"Transplacental hemorrhage in patients subjected to therapeutic abortion," by T. H. Parmley, et al. AMER J OBSTET GYNEC 106: 540-542, February 15, 1970.

WOMEN'S LIBERATION
see also: Laws & Legislation
         Sociology

"Abortion lib.," by J. Dingman. CHATELAINE 43:4, July, 1970.

"Freedom in family planning. The abortion law and women's liberation," by H. Muramatsu. JAP J MIDWIFE 24:10-19, December, 1970.

"It's alright, Ma (I'm only bleeding) (views on abortion,)" by Washington, D.C., Women's Liberation. MOTIVE 30:33-38, March, 1970.

"Out from under, women unite!" by K. Keate. SAT N 85:15-20, July, 1970.

"Whole world off her back: the Dorene Falk case," NEWSWEEK 75: 54-55, April 13, 1970.

"Will she, won't she?" by H. W. Ashworth. MANCHESTER MED GAZ 49:7, March, 1970.

"Women are turning on the heat," by G. Pape. MON TIMES 138: 46, June, 1970.

"Why women are *still* angry over abortion," by M. Gillen. CHATELAINE 43:34-35, 80+, October, 1970.

YOUTH
"Sequelae of artificial interruption of pregnancy in juveniles," by O. Mandausová, et al. CESK GYNEKOL 35:402-404, September, 1970

AUTHOR INDEX

Abolins, J. 26, 84
Adadevoh, B. K. 30, 52, 92
Adamo, S. J. 28, 103
Addison, P. H. 23, 83
Ananich, L. V. 29, 74
Anderson, D. 12, 81
Andrýs, J. 25, 65, 70
Arakaki, D. T. 16, 17, 54, 62, 106
Ardillo, L. 40, 53
Aronov, B. Kh. 26, 70
Arthure, H. G. 9, 80
Ashworth, H. W. 44, 118
Askrog, V. 38, 46
Atanasov, A. 14, 50, 68, 110
Aubertin, E. 26, 102
Aubry, R. H. 21, 66, 89
Aure, J. C. 43, 111, 116
Ayd, F. J., Jr. 5, 99

Bačič, M. 19, 56, 58
Bagrov, A. A. 35, 72, 109, 110
Baird, D. 4, 77
Bang, K. 25, 48, 109
Barmen, B. 43, 111, 116
Barnes, J. 21, 102
Barraya, P. L. 42, 92, 96
Baude, P. L. 15, 82
Beeson, T. 11, 81
Beïlin, A. L. 31, 97
Bein, D. 24, 75
Bendek, E. A. 42, 58, 73, 92

Bergsjo, P. 41, 58
Bernstein, G. S. 20, 51
Bickers, W. M. 23, 69
Bodiazhina, V. I. 18, 74
Boué, A. 5, 55
Boué, J. G. 13, 61, 106
Bowman, J. M. 41, 117
Boyce, R. M. 39, 86, 115
Bradley, J. G. 36, 98
Breen, J. L. 17, 47, 97, 108
Bréhant, J. 30, 85
Brodie, D. W. 28, 62
Brody, J. E. 8, 89, 100
Brown, B. F. 16, 28, 75, 76
Brown, J. B. 21, 28, 66, 89
Brown, N. K. 31, 103
Bruniquel, G. 28, 49
Brutar, V. 24, 69
Buckle, A. E. 43, 111, 116
Buckley, W. F., Jr. 12, 101
Buresh, B. 38, 91
Burke, C. 7, 78, 100
Burns, W. A. 35, 85
Butler, C. W. 33, 95, 113
Byrn, R. M. 8, 80

Caillouette, J. C. 30, 35, 57, 58, 98
Callahan, D. 15, 27, 53, 103
Cameron, W. J. 38, 73, 111
Carlton, M. A. 22, 87, 112
Carr, D. H. 13, 53, 62, 106

119

Case, W. 8, 54, 65, 80
Cashman, D. 9, 100
Cathely, M. 40, 63
Cavanagh, D. 33, 35, 85, 90, 98
Cerón, E. A. 6, 49
Chalupa, M. 32, 71, 109
Charlewood, G. P. 17, 47
Charvet, F. 12, 97
Chatfield, W. R. 29, 46
Chowdhury, N. N. 40, 115
Christakos, A. C. 19, 82, 112
Cisler, L. 8, 80
Clyne, D. G. 33, 104
Coffey, P. G. 39, 114
Cohen, J. 18, 50, 61, 62
Colucci, G. 21, 47, 64, 109
Connor, E. J. 39, 40, 76, 115
Conry, D. 10
Crawford, J. P. 4, 76
Csapo, A. I. 34, 50, 71, 93
Cullen, B. F. 18, 45, 65, 112

Dafoe, C. 14, 81, 90
Daily, E. F. 19, 59
David, H. P. 33, 59, 103
DeAluarez, R. R. 21, 63, 112
Deedy, J. 10, 101
Despodova, Ts. 34, 57, 64
Dhadial, R. K. 13, 60, 61, 105
Diggory, P. 4, 31, 85, 99
Dillon, S. 32, 57, 93
Dingman, J. 8, 25, 83, 118
Diviš, J. 24, 51, 69
Dlhoš, E. 18, 51, 68
Dodder, G. C., 7, 79
Don, N. V. 44, 105
Douglas, C. P. 42, 116
Downing, S. W. 9, 80
Dráč, P. 13, 31, 50, 62, 71, 106, 113
Draper, P. 34, 85

Drinan, R. F. 37, 104
Droegemueller, W. 25, 35, 57, 113, 114
Duffy, M. A. 11, 101
Dumont, M. 19, 31, 47, 48, 10:
Durieux, R. 55
Dvořák, M. 17, 64, 87
Dytrych, Z. 33, 103

Edwards, J. H. 42, 58
Edwards, R. F. 30, 57
Ekmen, H. 40, 46
Embrey, M. P. 18, 23, 69, 94
Enschede, C. J. 3
Eskes, T. K. 4, 55
Evans, D. 34, 76
Evans, J. H. 32, 55

Filshie, G. M. 40, 95, 116
Finger, H. 34, 92
Finnis, J. 5, 77
Fisher, B. E. 12, 81
Fitzgerald, J. A. 8, 79
Fleck, S. 37, 96
Flowers, C. E., Jr. 23, 41, 86, 102
Foglia, V. G. 20, 61
Ford, E. F. 37, 59, 104
Forrest, W. H., Jr. 18, 45, 112
Fortier, L. 29, 66
Freda, V. J. 40, 92
Freeman, G. 30, 67, 90
Fuchs, V. 24, 47

Galitskaia, S. A. 31, 48, 74
Gardner, R. F. R. 13, 101
Gellé, P. 32, 55, 67
Gendon, Z. Ia. 24, 49, 70, 109
Gibbs, F. J. 31, 55
Gillen, M. 44, 118
Gillespie, A. 22, 60, 107
Gillet, J. Y. 25, 64

Goldman, J. A. 41, 107, 116, 117
Goldsmith, S. 16, 82
Goodhart, C. B. 4, 5, 77, 99
Goodlin, R. C. 22, 30, 57, 71, 74, 117
Green, G. H. 20, 61
Greenhouse, L. J. 10, 15, 80, 82
Gregoire 40, 73
Griaznova, I. M. 42, 55, 87
Grisczenko, W. I. 37, 61
Grünfeld, B. 26, 84
Guerrero, R. 10, 60, 105, 108

Haffter, C. 20, 89
Halberstam, M. J. 9, 80
Hall, M. F. 26, 54, 102
Hall, R. E. 9, 41, 66, 105
Handru, M. 14, 51, 75
Hannaford, J. M. 6, 99
Harrison, C. P. 39, 115
Harwick, H. J. 27, 52, 88
Hauser, G. A. 13, 49, 66
Hay, D. 44, 117
Heczko, P. 24, 69
Heine, C. 3
Heller, A. 14, 81
Heller, L. 36, 98
Herndon, J. E. 34, 103, 113
Hershey, N. 5, 74, 99, 108
Hervet, E. 35, 104
Higier, J. 10, 25, 45, 65, 67, 69
Hingorani, V. 40, 117
Hirokawa, O. 12, 47
Ho, C. Y. 23, 46, 61, 106
Hodgson, J. E. 44, 91, 117
Holder, A. R. 7, 79
Honoré, M. 22, 74
Houdek, J. 36, 52, 72

Howells, J. G. 19, 82, 91
Howorka, E. 10, 33, 55, 57, 58, 65, 71
Hrazdil, K. 29, 46, 71
Hsu, L. Y. 29, 52, 63
Hughes, B. J. 11, 101
Hughes, J. H. 19, 54, 60, 107
Hyde, G. 4, 77

Irwin, T. 83
Isaacs, N. F. 5, 99
Iwata, M. 23, 112

Jakubowska, M. 46, 67
James, W. H. 26, 84, 102
Jensen, J. G. 43, 110, 111
Jenssen, H. 43, 111, 116
Jirátko, K. 37, 53, 73, 108
Johansson, E. D. B. 17, 56, 89, 112
John, A. H. 20, 60, 65, 112
Johnson, J. 39, 96, 114
Josey, W. E. 12, 46, 56, 97

Kadotani, T. 3, 61, 105
Karim, S. M. 32, 39, 42, 60, 94, 95, 106, 107, 115, 116
Karpel, C. 22, 102
Kaskarelis, D. 38, 48, 110
Keate, K. 29, 118
Keemer, E. B., Jr. 26, 102
Kenealy, W. J. 28, 76
Kestelman, P. 33, 90
Khidirbeil, Kh. A. 13, 49, 96
Khvat, E. I. 43, 98
Kimball, C. P. 37, 59, 114
Kirkels, V. G. 4, 61
Knapp, R. D., Jr. 36, 104
Kohoutek, F. 36, 53, 72
Kohoutek, M. 25, 31, 36, 54, 70, 72, 76, 107
Koike, K. 16, 62, 63

Kokoszka, W. 18, 47, 87
Kolářová, O. 26, 27, 51, 70,
   95, 102, 107
Kopečný, J. 23, 31, 49, 57, 64,
   69, 89
Kotásek, A. 28, 36, 46, 52, 70,
   72
Koukal, J. 24, 54, 69
Kovács, L. 34, 57, 61, 114
Křikal, Z. 36, 72
Kronus, R. 43, 53, 73
Kundsin, R. B. 35, 88

Lader, L. 27, 84
Landgreen, M. 25, 85
Laně, V. 36, 53, 72, 87
Lange, R. 26, 86
Larson, S. L. 13, 62
Láska, L. 22, 69
Lebensohn, Z. M. 39, 115
Le Coz, A. 56, 74, 92
Lee, S. 36, 72, 107
Legrain, M. 32, 55, 92
LeRoux, R. 3
Levene, H. I. 25, 83, 95, 113
Lewis, A. C. 39, 111, 114
Lewis, T. L. 21, 63
Liley, A. W. 19, 68
Lindelius, R. 38, 86
Linton, E. B. 3, 89
Lipinski, A. 12, 60
Litwak, O. 19, 60, 106
Locardi, G. 29, 57, 63, 89,
   98

MacGregor, C. 17, 63
MacNeil, E. 37, 104
Machanik, G. 6, 91
Mackú, F. 27, 28, 52, 70
Maeots, K. 5, 99
Mahon, R. 43, 105
Manabe, Y. 30, 71, 93

Mandausová, O. 36, 52, 72,
   118
Marcel, J. E. 32, 90
Marder, L. 32, 33, 85, 95, 103
   113
Margolis, A. J. 14, 26, 84, 11
Martynshin, M. Ia. 18, 49, 56,
   87
Massett, L. 7, 79
Matsuura, T. 31, 38, 63, 76,
   104
Matz, R. 14, 101
Maxwell, J. W. 14, 108
McCance, C. 8, 90, 100
McDonald, R. 42, 116
McEwan, J. 4, 76, 89
McGarry, J. M. 20, 110
McGowan, G. W. 12, 47
McKie, B. 5, 77
Mega, M. 40, 50, 117
Mentasti, P. 56, 66, 93
Mikamo, K. 10, 50, 61, 105
Miller, J. R. 43, 53
Miranda, L. S. 16, 101
Montanari, G. D. 40, 58, 94
Moore, J. L., Jr. 9, 20, 83, 1C
   107
Morgentaler, H. 3
Morra, C. 21, 56, 66, 68, 93
Moyers, T. G. 7, 79, 100
Mukherji, S. 17, 68, 91
Muller, C. F. 21, 59
Muramatsu, H. 20, 59, 118
Murdzhiev, A. 20, 51
Murray, S. 41, 117
Murrell, P. J. 26, 84

Nadler, H. L. 19, 60, 112
Nagauchi, K. 19, 45, 68
Naib, Z. M. 11, 50, 105
Német, J. 31, 71, 110
Németi, S. 11, 87, 93

Nesit, V. 22, 43, 51, 53, 68, 73

Neubauer, G. 41, 117

Newman, S. J. 87, 105

Niemineva, K. 32, 87

Niiazova, M. A. 38, 48, 109

Nusch, W. 17, 54

O'Leary, J. A. 37, 106

O'Neill, R. T. 14, 22, 51, 97, 106

Onishi, Y. 18, 68, 108

Ostergard, D. R. 14, 35, 56, 97, 98

Packwood, B. 85

Padeh, B. 13, 62, 106

Padovec, J. 20, 83

Páez, L. E. S. 23

Pape, G. 44, 118

Pare, C. M. 22, 112

Parmley, T. H. 41, 116, 118

Pasini, W. 42, 92, 95

Pearse, W. H. 39, 115

Penev, I. 27, 48, 87

Peng, J. Y. 27, 54

Perretti, F. 42, 53, 73

Perrin, L. E. 42, 97

Peterson, M. L. 15, 60, 107

Pettersson, F. 13, 101

Pfanner, D. 38, 111, 114

Pfeiffer, E. 33, 95, 113

Philippe, E. 18, 30, 51, 52, 63, 106

Phillips, D. F. 6, 67, 78

Pilpel, H. 11, 81

Pion, R. J. 9, 74, 92

Pohlman, E. 6, 99

Pond, D. A. 39, 86, 115

Pontuch, A. 30, 71

Potts, D. M. 39, 114

Presl, J. 22, 109

Quinn, J. R. 34, 104

Rageth, S. 23, 47

Ramsey, P. R. 9, 19, 75, 100, 101

Ramirez, O. V. 28, 67, 107

Rarick, J. R. 36, 85

Ratten, G. J. 26, 109

Remsberg, C. 36, 85

Resnik, H. L. P. 5, 99

Ribeiro, L. 26, 84, 90

Richardson, P. A. 4, 67

Richon, J. 47

Roberts, G. 10, 94

Rosen, H. 6, 78

Rössner, P. 12, 47

Roth-Brandel, U. 32, 94, 113

Roussel, C. 10, 55

Roux, C. 27, 52, 62

Roy, W. R. 8, 90

Rozovskii, I. S. 21, 64

Rugiati, S. 13, 62, 63

Rushton, D. I. 37, 63

Russell, K. P. 34, 57, 96

Ruzicska, P. 16, 62

Sachs, F. L. 27, 98

Sadovsky, E. 31, 57, 64, 89

Sakurabayashi, M. 41, 58, 93

Salasc, J. 35, 52

Salvi, F. 25, 64

Salzman, L. 28, 76

Sanders, M. K. 34, 76, 114

Sandoval, J. B. 21, 66

Santamarina, B. A. 35, 41, 58, 98

Sapák, K. 43, 48, 73

Sasu, S. 23, 69

Savage, A. 17, 101

Schoenberg, C. 4, 59

Schulman, H. 23, 69

Sem-Jacobsen, C. W. 18, 101

Senay, E. C. 39, 50, 115
Serova, T. A. 11, 74
Shaalan, M. K. 37, 48
Shainess, N. 6, 100
Shinagawa, N. 24, 110
Silverman, M. 33, 64, 103
Simakova, M. G. 12, 92, 96
Simms, M. 7, 78
Simon, N. M. 33, 96, 113
Skála, V. 36, 52, 72
Skjaeraasen, J. S. 13, 49, 56
Slatin, M. 40
Smith, E. B. 78
Smith, K. D. 38, 114
Smith, R. G. 30, 85, 90
Snortland, N. 7, 79
Soiva, K. 25, 85
Sokolik, L. 21, 51, 68
Sood, S. V. 14, 49
Southgate, M. T. 41, 105
Spanio, P. 23, 41, 58, 94,
  117
Sprague, C. 35, 96, 106, 114
Sparkes, R. S. 24, 62
Springer, A. 20, 51
Squire, R. 22, 83, 102
Stack, J. M. 7, 79
Stallworthy, J. 34, 39, 104,
  115
Stratford, B. F. 3, 50
Strom, A. 10, 80
Sturma, J. 32, 59
Suganuma, T. 37, 38, 91, 104
Sullivan, P. R. 35, 104, 114
Sussman, W. 20, 90, 112
Suter, H. H. 30, 91
Suter, P. E. 42, 111
Sutin, J. B. 28, 76
Szemesi, I. 11, 88, 97
Szereday, Z. 29, 54, 71

Tausk, M. 21, 66

Taymor, M. L. 7, 78
Teilmann, H. 6, 78
Testart, J. 30, 65, 92
Thompson, H. 39, 115
Tietze, C. 8, 40, 59, 74, 91,
  100, 116
Tinelli, L. 11, 56, 63, 88
Truninger, E. 8, 79
Tsutsumi, N. 27, 103
Tuchmann-Duplessis, H. 11, 6

Vácha, K. 11, 67, 91
Vago, O. 11, 50, 65, 68
Vainberg, I. A. 35, 46, 72
Valvanne, L. 20, 101
Velasco, V. R. 17, 35, 54, 10
Vido, I. 25, 70, 113
Vincent, C. E. 5, 99

Waldeyer, L. 44, 73
Wallner, H. 16, 74
Walsh, J. J. 41, 116, 117
Walter, G. S. 33, 96
Wawryk, R. 20, 24, 38, 42, 48,
  54, 110
Weber, P. J. 30, 103
Weidenbach, A. 23, 51
Weise, W. 16, 68, 110
Weiss, G. 17, 75, 88
Wetrich, D. W. 40, 116
Whittington, H. G. 18, 95, 112
Wierstakow, B. 66, 111
Wiest, W. G. 30, 71, 93
Williamson, N. W. 7, 79
Wiqvist, N. 23, 39, 69, 94,
  113, 115
Worsnop, L. R. 7, 78
Wurm, R. S. 3, 77

Yoshikawa, T. 43, 86

Zachary, R. B. 9, 100

Zák, K. 27, 52, 70
Zanden, F. W. 44
Zdímalová, M. 38, 73, 76
Zimmerman, D. R. 22, 90
Zorlescu, I. 37, 97
Zozaya, F. J. A. 14, 75
Zwinger, A. 38, 53, 64, 109